CW00823339

Nicolaj Højer Nielsen

STARTUP FUNDING

Contents

Acknowledgements

This book wouldn't have been possible without the help and input from a lot of people who I encouraged to read its first (very bad!) drafts, and who provided cases, valuable feedback, and suggestions.

I would therefore like to thank:

Junaid Ahmad; Cristobal Alonso; Tommy Andersen; Hemant Aneja; Thor Angelo, Ioanei Andrei; Julien Andrieux; Thor Angelo; Søren Anker Nielsen; Reinis Andersons; Thor Ansbæk; Frederik Balslev; Tarek Besbes; Casper Blom; Janek Borgmann; Kasper Brandi Petersen; Jakob Bruhns; Lars Buch; Line Byrfelt Grønlykke; Alessandro Colombo; Per Diemer; Jean-Paul Delimat; James Draper; Dan Eisenhardt, Morten Elk; Simon Egenfeldt-Nielsen; Bjarke Finlov; Morten Flatau; Gustav Friis; Jimmy Fussing Nielsen; Shomit Ghose; Tomasz Gidzgier; Reuben Greet-Smith; Peter Guy; Marwan el-Hakim; Niklas Hall; Morten Høgholm Pedersen; Justin Holley; Hiram Ip; Peter Jackson; Debbie Jenkins; Marc Leplay; Lisa Long; Nils Mandrup; Søren Mayland; Monique Meulemans; Jesús Otero; Nini Oy; Kannan Palaniswamy; Christian Podojstersek; Stefan Raff; Niels Henrik Rasmussen; Kasper Refskou; Denis Rivin; Henrik Rosendahl; Kristian Schwarz Larsen; Amir Schlachet; Magnus Schückes; Dale Shelton; Jacob Simonsen; Franco Soldera; Morten Sørensen; Torben Sparre; Johan Stockmarr; Federico Suria; Nicolas de Teilmann; Christian Thaler-Wolski; Arne Tonning; Lone Veng; Andrew Ward; Chady Zein; Henrik Zillmer; and Chun Zhong.

 © 2017 Nicolaj Højer Nielsen

Preface

This book is written for entrepreneurs who are wondering how they can get the necessary funding for their startup.

Maybe you're having a hard time finding investors, or you're planning to start a business but have no idea where to look for investment. I'm eager to help entrepreneurs get funding, bring their great business ideas to life, and scale them.

I know how entrepreneurs like you think. And how investors think. I've been in your entrepreneurial shoes, as I've been involved in startups for almost 20 years – both as a founder *and* as an investor, meaning I've seen it from both sides. I want to help you avoid the mistakes I made – and I've made them all. I've looked for funding in the wrong places, and counted the money before we had it. So I know how it feels to be you, as an entrepreneur with dreams and a great idea. I also know how it feels to be approached by you, as an investor, and that unless you send investors like me the right material, at the right time, with your great idea de-risked and bootstrapped, we won't fund you.

About Nicolaj Højer Nielsen

Nicolaj Højer Nielsen is a serial entrepreneur and business angel who has been building startups since 1999. He focuses on high potential startups, and has co-founded and invested in 13 companies, primarily within IT.

He has experience of securing funding from all possible sources – friends and family, business angels, venture capital funds and public funds. His experience is based on reviewing thousands of different investment opportunities and he knows the fundraising process from both sides of the table.

His latest venture is Copenhagen United, an investment fund focusing on providing capital and mentoring for early-stage software companies.

Nicolaj dedicates a significant part of his time to help other startups. He lectures on entrepreneurship at Copenhagen Business School, and also coaches entrepreneurs. Nicolaj also holds an MBA from INSEAD.

 © 2017 Nicolaj Højer Nielsen

Introduction

There are often stories in the media about entrepreneurs and startups that went on to become very successful *after* having been turned down by banks and investors. Those stories and the stories entrepreneurs tell me about banks and investors all point to the same things: banks behave like banks and investors behave like investors. Most entrepreneurs don't realise this and seek funding in the wrong places and at the wrong time, mainly because they don't understand how investors and banks think!

Knowing who you are dealing with is key to a successful deal. This is also true when you're making a deal with a bank or an investor!

To know someone is to know how they think, and knowing how people think involves learning about what drives their decisions. Most entrepreneurs think in terms of ideas because the idea they have for a startup project drives and energises them. Their idea is the projection of their vision; it's like a pair of glasses through which they view the world.

The majority of investors *don't* think in terms of ideas. Actually, most investors believe that the value of a business idea is very limited – it is the actions <u>after</u> the initial idea is created that generate value. Investors and banks think in terms of risk and return on investment. They accept and operate with different levels of risk. To a bank or an investor, an idea is nothing but a risk, and that's exactly why many entrepreneurs can't get funding for their business idea.

❝By reading this book you will learn how investors think. Thinking like an investor will make you a more successful entrepreneur!❞

An idea (no matter how good it may seem) is 100% risk. Of course, both banks and investors will say no to funding your idea. They have to.

There's a lot of talk about the funding gap facing early-stage startups, but this is mainly caused by the thought gap that exists between funders and entrepreneurs – the gap most startups fall into.

If entrepreneurs better understood how banks and investors think, they would realise the futility of pitching a project to them in its early stages. And when the time came to actually pitch, they would be better prepared and have a much better chance of securing funding.

This book is about building understanding and preparing entrepreneurs for pitching their project to investors. It's also about what entrepreneurs need to do in order to develop and de-risk their startup project enough for it to become attractive to professional investors.

Chapter 1:
Do you really need external funding?

The if, when, and where to look for funding is dependent on the type of startup you're creating. You will learn to identify the characteristics of each type of company and understand the implications for your funding strategy. Broadly speaking, there are three different startup scenarios.

Type 1: You don't need external funding!

Some companies don't need external funding. They have limited funding needs, typically because the product can be launched and generate revenue quickly. Match that with limited sales and marketing costs, and you can end up in the perfect situation of not needing external funding for your startup.

For example, if you decided to start a consulting company, your initial startup needs are limited: a computer, an office space and an internet connection and you're up and running. You hope for customers from day one, but even in the worst-case scenario, where it takes you a few months to get your first customers, your needs should be covered by your savings.

If that's you, great! You don't need to worry about how to get your company funded and can focus your energy on running and growing your business!

Case study: Casper Blom – how to start a business at 12 years old with no funding

My granddad was visiting us one day when I was around 12 years old. He noticed I was interested in and had a flair for buying/selling cheap stuff, and asked if I could get him some cheap golf balls. I had no clue about golf balls, but said I'd give it a try!

I did some market research. Pretty fast I realised the margins on new golf balls were very bad, and I needed cash if I was going to build up a stock of imported golf balls. I had to look for another approach. I then came across the US phenomenon of *lake balls* – golf balls that have been shot into lakes by mistake and then fished up and sold as used. This sounded interesting, so I started researching the Danish market. There were a few vendors, but no large ones. All the

 © 2017 Nicolaj Højer Nielsen

companies were driven as part time shops, and had web pages that I thought I could do much better. I emptied my piggy bank (€40) and thought this was enough for me to get some second-hand golf balls to resell. I then called a lot of golf clubs and made a deal with one that allowed me to pick up the lake balls for free. At the same time I made an agreement with a scuba diver who would get the balls out of the lake for me for €0.15 a ball.

I then sold the golf balls to my granddad for €0.30 a ball. That gave me a nice profit of €0.15 a ball (VAT, income tax etc. wasn't included in my calculations). I then started selling the lake balls to other golf players and it started to look more and more like a real but small company.

Then in 2007, when I was 15, I decided to take my business online and bought an internet domain (www.billigegolfbolde.dk). Initially, it was just a very simple site with a contact form where you could order golf balls. Later I got external developers to make a professional web shop for me, and to this day the business is running on the same web shop. Fast forward to 2014, where the online shop is the largest vendor of golf balls in Denmark. It's expanded with other products for golfers, but its core business and revenue is still made up of used golf balls.

My advice to aspiring entrepreneurs looking at business ideas that can be realised without huge sums of funding is that they should start doing it now! Start building your business without looking for external investors and fancy business plans. Many potential entrepreneurs make starting a business overly complicated. Often you can do it relatively simply and quickly from your own funds. Later, when your business is up and running, you might want to expand and can then look for investors.

Type 2: You need funding to get the startup off the ground

Let's say you have an idea that will take you three or four years to develop into a real product. In a perfect world, your customers would pay up front, but in this not-so-perfect world you'll need financing. In other words, without external funding you won't have a company.

This kind of company can be exemplified by a group of university students starting up in the university laboratory with an idea for a biotech company that produces a new type of medicine that can cure cancer. The lab isn't that expensive for them as they have the resources they need. At some point, however, they have to go all-in and test the drug and dedicate more resources to research and development. To put it into perspective, the total costs could easily add up to several hounded million euros before the drug is on the market.

This is the case for most research and development intensive projects. Of course, if you are a biotech company you might be able to sign a licensing agreement with a potential buyer a few years into development so you don't have to fund the hundred million euros yourself. You only have to fund a few million euros. Of course, that's still a lot to most people!

So for some companies funding is the only option. Either you get funding for your startup, or there will be no company. The question to ask is when and from which sources to secure the cash needed to build your company.

Case study: MotilityCount – getting funding for a sperm quality home test

In 2009 two experienced researchers, Jacob Mollenbach and Steen Laursen, from the human fertility field came up with a new concept: They wanted to make a home test for sperm quality so men could get an answer about potential infertility problems in the comfort of their own home, without having to visit a fertility clinic. They did some experiments with a prototype that showed promising results, and in 2010 invited Nicolaj Højer Nielsen to join the company to strengthen the team on the commercial side. They also prepared and sent in the first patent application to protect their concept from future imitators. Nicolaj Højer Nielsen explains:

The main obstacle to proceeding was money. The estimated cost of finalising development, testing prototypes, starting production and regulatory work was around €1.5 million - much more than three struggling entrepreneurs had in their own pockets. Getting external funding was the only viable option if we were to proceed.

We quickly decided NOT to try to raise the entire amount from day one. Instead, we aimed to raise the first €500,000, which would be sufficient to finalise development and generate enough data to show our device actually worked. After months of meetings, in 2011 we convinced a public support fund and four friends to invest in the company. Then followed two years of trial and error (with over 50 different 3D-printed prototypes) until we finally had a device that was as accurate and easy to use as we wanted. In 2013 with this data, we raised the €1 million needed from local business angels, our manufacturing partner, and a public support fund to get the device manufactured and regulatory approval for sale.

Fast forward to the end of 2016. The product, under the name SwimCount, is now sold online (www.swimcount.com) and at pharmacies worldwide in collaboration with lo-

 © 2017 Nicolaj Højer Nielsen

cal distributors. But this brings a new dilemma: should the company raise more money (for sales/marketing spending) to try to grow the business faster, or should it grow more slowly based on the cash flow generated by the business? As a company Motility-Count therefore went from a *Type 2: Without funding there is no company* to a *Type 3: Without funding there's no growth.*

Type 3: Without funding there's no growth

The third subgroup of startups is, in theory, able to fund the startup themselves but might consider getting external funding to drive further growth.

One example is a startup where the upfront development cost is relatively low, for example, developing a simple, consumer-oriented smartphone app with a development cost of €25,000 or so to cover code and getting it into app stores.

The revenue model for most consumer apps is that the basic app is low priced or completely free. To succeed you need lots of downloads and a premium version for converting some of the downloads into paying users – which is also what your competitors are looking to do. As an app developer you have two choices: either you continue small scale using word of mouth, social media marketing and funding it all yourself, or you go big. Let's say you've invented a brilliant app, everything is going well and you've gained loads of local PR and users. However, before you know it the market is flooded with competing apps looking to steal your market position.

One option is to take funding to scale your business, develop a better version and storm the market. If you go it alone with no external funding and slow growth rates, your market position may be overtaken by aggressive, well-funded competitors.

For this type of startup, the question is not therefore whether you can manage the startup without funding, but if you can get necessary customer growth without such funding. And if you don't accept funding, will you be able to survive in the long term?

Case study: Secunia – decided not to take growth capital

Deciding whether to take in capital to further grow your business is not an easy choice as explained in the case of Secunia below:

In 2002, serial entrepreneur Niels Henrik Rasmussen decided to create an IT-security company with four business partners. They wanted to develop a product that could help companies prevent exploitation of software vulnerabilities. Niels Henrik Rasmussen explains:

From our inception in 2002 we were focused on building a great business despite all odds, being bootstrapped and having competitors that had raised over US $10 million. We started off with just $26,000 and a salary pay slip of zero for the first 18 months. Back then IT-security business valuations were low after the IT bubble burst. So we wanted to build a better business case through a strong and healthy business discipline, and we focused on agile development of our services and gaining market traction. We cultivated this over the years, having strong growth year after year in our revenues and earnings.

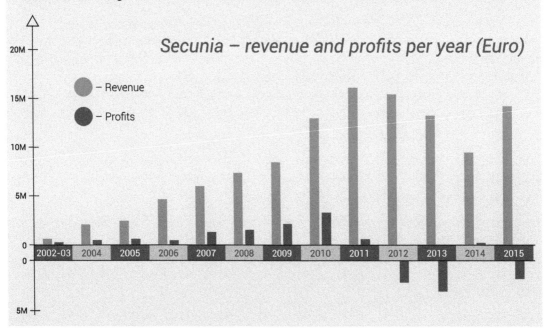

Secunia – revenue and profits per year (Euro)

In 2004, and again in 2005, we discussed bringing in external investors to provide growth capital in the €2-3 million range, but decided to pursue the upcoming challenges on our own terms and grow organically with our own funds. Again, over the following years we were approached and offered growth capital. Same answer – we believed we could go further and faster on our own. Over the years our organisation grew to more than 140 employees of 21 different nationalities at our peak. As we progressed towards 2010, several exit opportunities presented to us. However, we didn't want to pursue them as our business was doing great and we were having fun developing the organisation. Instead of selling our company completely, we decided to accept an offer from a capital fund where we initially sold 30% of the shares in 2010 and later sold our remaining shares in 2013.

Should we have taken investors in early instead of growing the company organically? This is a hard question. At that time we didn't want to, not only due to dilution (less ownership), but also because we would then have lost control of the business.

Take-away points

Do you really need funding to get the business off the ground? Many companies actually don't, and if you're in that lucky situation, you should focus on building your business and not pitching to investors!

Some startups do need funding since their upfront costs are so high it may be unrealistic to finance it with your own money. Others need funding to grow the company.

In the following chapters we look at the different types of investors, which startups they might be interested in, at which stages they invest, and how to convince them to fund your company. But first let's look at how investors evaluate startups in terms of risk and reward.

Chapter 2

Your startup's
risk/reward profile

To maximise the chances of your fundraising process being successful, you need to under-stand how investors and other funding sources like banks think, and thereby avoid the understanding gap that too many startups fall into when searching for funding. This includes learning how they think in terms of the risk/reward profile of the investment opportunity you present to them.

The investor matrix

Startups can have very different risk profiles and also different levels of potential reward if they're successful. From a potential investment case perspective, and in investors' eyes, this makes them very different from each other.

The risk/reward profile of your startup is best illustrated using the investor matrix model; a simple 2x2 diagram as shown below. Risk is on one axis and reward on the other. Any company can be placed on the matrix, showing high or low return and high or low risk. It's a simple tool investors indirectly use when evaluating investment opportunities.

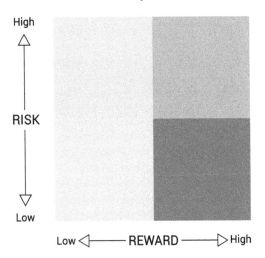

Let's look at two cases which illustrate this difference – one with low risk/low reward and another with high risk/high reward:

Low risk/low reward: Local e-commerce website. An entrepreneur with a simple e-commerce website would be perceived as low risk/low reward. Why? Because it's really hard to convince anyone you will be the next Amazon. Consumers will compare prices across different online retailers, and this normally results in relatively low margins, a limited market size for simple e-commerce sites, and low rewards for the investor. The risk is relatively low because you aren't inventing a new product or putting a million euros into research and development. You're just distributing a product from another manufacturer which carries relatively little risk.

Another example is Casper Blom's used golf balls website mentioned earlier. It's hardly the next billion euro company, but since he's already proved there's a market for his product and

 © 2017 Nicolaj Højer Nielsen

he can sell it at a profit, the perceived risk is also low.

High risk/high reward: Biotech company. At the opposite end of the continuum we find the biotech archetype startup. Perhaps this is two researchers coming out of university with initial research for the cure for malaria. If they succeed in developing a vaccine, they will have a drug that sells for billions of euros and a company worth a multiplier of those billions of euros. A high reward product. But the risk? The chance that anything invented in a lab will become a marketable drug is very small. Typically, the chance of commercial success is less than one per cent. Investors know this and know that it will cost millions of euros in development. It's a classic high risk/high reward product.

Your risk/reward profile determines what type of investor will invest and when. Some investors are looking for the next Google/Facebook with an enormous financial return (which most often also comes with a high risk), while others aren't willing to take the same amount of risk but are OK with a lower financial upside. Many founders make the serious mistake of thinking that all investors are looking for high return/high risk startups. But there are just as many financing options available for low risk/low reward startups.

 Key note: Which risk/reward are you offering?

A low financial opportunity doesn't mean you won't find any investors – but the type of investor interested in your startup is most likely very different from an investor looking to invest in the next Facebook. Your first job is to understand which case you have on your hands and which type of investor you need to approach and when.

Next we will investigate further what determines the risk/reward profile of your startup so you will have a better understanding of how an investor will evaluate it.

The factors that determine your risk/reward profile

The risk/reward profile of your startup is determined by four key factors:

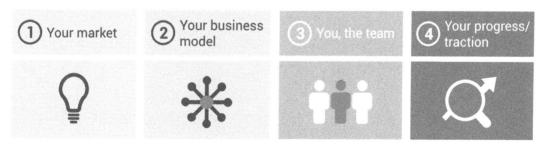

1. Your market

The industry you're in and the product you will make are key to determining your project's risk/reward profile. Some industries have a higher risk of failure than others, but hopefully also a higher financial outcome if you succeed. Different industries therefore attract different types of investors!

Examples of markets perceived high risk versus low risk by most investors:

LOW RISK	HIGH RISK
Import/export business	Pharmaceuticals/biotech
E-commerce websites	Consumer apps/software
Consulting/professional services	Consumer electronics/hardware
Physical retail shops	Most technology-based university inventions

A misunderstanding among many founders is that the risk/reward profile is ONLY impacted by the industry you're competing in and the product you offer. This isn't the case. Your business model, who you are, and the progress/traction your startup has achieved impact the perceived risk/reward from the investor's point of view.

2. Your business model

You can develop different business models that significantly affect the risk/reward levels to better suit your own appetite for risk versus reward, as well as use different business models to attract different types of investors.

Example 1: Software startup

MARKET	LOW RISK/LOW REWARD	HIGH RISK/HIGH REWARD
SOFTWARE	Consulting (selling hours)	Product (making/selling software)
BIOTECH	Consulting, joint venture, early-stage licensing	Developing own intellectual property/ patents, developing pharmaceuticals, doing clinical trials

Imagine a group of software engineers working at a big consulting company. One day they might think: *Hey, why are we only getting a low salary compared to the high prices our employer is charging for our services to corporate clients? We can do this ourselves! We have contact with companies wanting to buy our services! Let's start our own small consulting company!*

 © 2017 Nicolaj Højer Nielsen

This is a classic low reward/low risk business model. Most likely the engineers will actually make a higher salary at their new company with limited risk. The biggest risk is that they don't get the expected number of clients (especially at the beginning), but after they've built their network and reputation there will be limited risk. The business model doesn't involve putting money in any physical stock or any upfront development work. The customers will pay by the hour or per project, and this of course involves some risk of customers not paying their bills. But compared with most other business models the risk is limited – and so is the financial, long-term reward. The company's income is directly linked to the number of hours it invoices (no passive income), and in most cases the selling price for such companies (unless they become very big) is also relatively low. So investors will perceive such companies as low risk/low reward and they will therefore appeal to a specific type of investor. The funding need of such a company is also limited, so there's a good chance they don't need external investors.

But imagine the same group of software engineers starting a very different type of business in the same industry: *Why don't we start a company that builds a piece of standard software for industry X, which we will sell at a monthly subscription per customer instead of us having to build customised software solutions for each customer? We can sell the software to many customers, which means much less work involved since we are selling the same piece of plug-n-play software to each customer.* This is a very different company. Most likely they will have to put in months or years of development work before they get their first customer. And it's likely they will need more funding before they have enough customers to pay their bills. In other words – high risk. But it also gives the company a higher potential reward because, if it's successful, the company owning the rights to this popular piece of software could be worth much more than the same group of engineers selling their services on a per-hour basis.

Example 2: Biotech startup

A biotech startup is by definition very high risk and high reward. If you follow the traditional business model of raising venture capital to develop and test your own pharmaceutical compounds (because the chance of ending up with an approved and commercially successful drug is less than one per cent), the cost of up to one billion euros for doing so must be offset by an opportunity for creating a company worth billions of euros.

This is a high risk/high reward opportunity, but there are other opportunities. You can use alternative business models that will both change the risk/reward profile of your startup and the amount of funding needed to realise your startup project.

Such an alternative business model could be where researchers team up with existing pharma/biotech companies instead of building a new company from scratch. This model could take many forms – from selling patents to the other company, to selling hours/consulting, to joint ventures. This will most likely result in the opportunity (reward) getting smaller (you no longer have the opportunity to create a billion euro company), and it will also significantly reduce the risk both for you as entrepreneur and for potential investors. Therefore, these alternative business models not only impact the risk/reward profile and the amount of funding needed but also determine who would be the most appropriate investor.

- -

(!) Key note: Which business model is best for you – the high or low risk model?

The key factor in determining this is YOU. And when you have decided which kind of company (and business model) you dream of making, you will also know the perceived risk/reward profile of the business, and therefore which fundraising sources are most relevant to you.

- -

3. You and your team

Who you are has a huge impact not only on the perceived risk but also the perceived upside (reward) in the mind of the investor.

Let's take one example. Assume that you pitch your mobile game project to an investor. Most likely the investor will think 'ultra-high risk' since statistics show that only a very small fraction of mobile games launched in app stores ever become profitable.

But then imagine your first slide in the pitch deck is about your team where you have people, on both the commercial and technical side, who have successfully launched mobile games before. This totally changes the perceived risk and reward!

Case study: Mofibo – why the CEO was the only reason the venture capital (VC) fund invested

In 2010 the entrepreneur Morten Strunge was on the lookout for venture funding for his next project. He had previously started and exited a very successful mobile telecom company but now wanted to enter the e-book market with his new company, Mofibo. He ended up in talks with the Danish, early-stage, venture capital fund SEED Capital, where Jakob Ekkelund was working as investment manager.

Jakob Ekkelund explains why he decided to invest in Mofibo:

When we decided to invest in Mofibo it was

actually despite a lot of things: I didn't really like the business model, the product wasn't launched and there was no validation of customer interest other than gut feeling. On top of this, there were several potential issues with the cost side of the business since there were very high variable costs related to purchase of the books from publishers. So why did we end up investing in Mofibo? The answer is very simple – the founder and CEO of the company was the well-known local entrepreneur Morten Strunge. I had followed Morten and was very impressed by the way he had run (and exited) his previous company, a mobile phone company. I guessed that Morten, with his experience in building great teams and adjusting his business model according to market response, could do it again – despite all the questions related to the business. Without Morten as CEO I would one hundred percent never have invested in Mofibo.

I totally understand, but knowing that investors prefer to work together with experienced entrepreneurs doesn't suddenly make me a successful serial entrepreneur. Of course not, but even first-time entrepreneurs have to realise that absolutely the most important element in the investor's analysis of your business proposal is the quality of your team. So BEFORE approaching investors you have to gather as strong a team as possible because this has a huge impact on your ability to get funding.

4. Your progress/traction

The final element that determines the perceived risk/reward of your project is how far along you are in the process. The same project (market + business model + team) will change significantly as you go along!

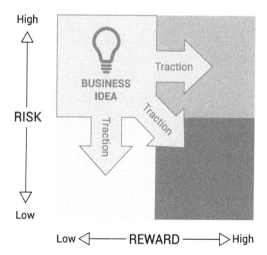

Most projects are low reward/high risk when you're at the ideas stage! Statistics show that only a few startups make it all the way from an idea to a successful business.

Many things can go wrong in the process. Maybe you don't manage to get a great team. Maybe you aren't able to build a great product. And at that idea stage (with no customers), it's hard to argue that you will attract a lot of customers.

But progress (or 'traction' in popular startup jargon) changes all this! Imagine the above idea for a mobile app game. Maybe they didn't get investors at the ideas stage because the investors didn't believe they were able to pull it off. But maybe they were able to develop and launch the game anyway. If done successfully, this progress/traction changes everything. Results from real products/users beats every type of forecast!

Case study: Autobutler – the law of attraction for startup funding

Founded in Denmark in 2010, Autobutler is one of Europe's leading online marketplaces for auto repairs, offering car owners an easy way to get quotes from garages. It currently has a network of garages and customers in Denmark, Sweden, UK and Germany. Peter Michael Oxholm Zigler, co-founder of Autobutler, explains:

In the initial phases of Autobutler's entrepreneurial journey, we had a really hard time raising money. That said we weren't really trying to raise funds for the first six months. We did meet up with a few angels, angel networks and seed investment funds, but it turned out to be a waste of time. And they all turned us down. Why? Because we were inexperienced at building businesses and raising money and had nothing but an unproven idea. We basically had no product, no money, and no process to get there, so the risk was too high.

After some serious focus on building a simple product, we had some initial traction with a beta launch of our product in Denmark, and very solid media coverage through our own PR efforts. We were suddenly in a better position to talk to angels. A few angels started to show interest and we pursued them all. Some lost interest, but we managed to keep three interested and played them against each other. In other words, we slowly began to understand how to play the fundraising game.

 © 2017 Nicolaj Højer Nielsen

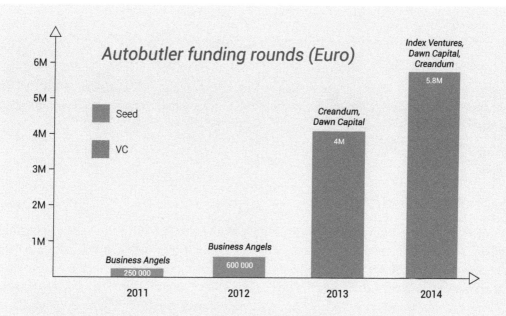

Autobutler funding rounds (Euro)

- Seed
- VC

6M
5M
4M
3M
2M
1M

Business Angels
250 000
2011

Business Angels
600 000
2012

Creandum,
Dawn Capital
4M
2013

Index Ventures,
Dawn Capital,
Creandum
5.8M
2014

It's the law of attraction. Once you become interesting, everybody wants to dance. On that note, we closed our first angel raise after approximately 16 months – and raised €235,000 in that round.

The traction in the market (growing number of users) we were able to create from our first angel investment suddenly made us more interesting to VCs, who started to open their doors. However, they were still a bit reluctant since we hadn't yet proved the (international) scalability. Again, we had to refocus on building the business so we opened up in the Swedish market and showed immediate traction and performance that was two or three times better than the Danish case.

This early adoption to the Swedish market completely turned the tables. All of a sudden we were perceived as a digital player, operating in a huge potential market space that had shown proof of concept and scalability. We were literally hunted down by national and international professional investors—the law of attraction again. We had the upper hand and could play hard to get – ultimately defining our own value to a certain extent.

That resulted in a Series A round with Creandum (VC fund) opening up the German market, followed by a Series B round with Index Ventures (another VC fund) scaling into the UK market. We were on a roll.

Eventually, PSA (the company that owns Peugeot and Citroën) saw the potential and the strategic fit with their corporate strategy, resulting in them acquiring the majority of the company in August 2016.

Key note: You contact investors too early

The main reason entrepreneurs are not able to attract investors is NOT because of 'bad' ideas but because they contact investors too early in the project when the perceived risk is much higher than the perceived reward.

Take-away points

Investors evaluate startups according to perceived risk (high/low) and perceived reward (high/low), and they are diverse in what they're looking for. Not all are searching for the next Facebook (which almost always comes with high risk), and many are OK with a much lower potential upside if you can argue that the risk is also lower. Your startup's risk/reward level is not only related to the industry you're in but also your chosen business model and team, and the perceived risk/reward profile changes greatly as you progress with the project.

The main reason many entrepreneurs fail to raise funding is not due to 'bad ideas' but because they approach the wrong type of investors at the wrong point in time, before they achieved any 'traction' to show to the investors. Traction beats everything!

 © 2017 Nicolaj Højer Nielsen

© 2017 Nicolaj Højer Nielsen

———— Chapter 3: ————

Who invests in what and when

Let's now go into more detail and analyse which type of investors are interested in different types of projects and at which phase they might be interested in your project.

What do investors look for?

In the investor matrix below, the different types of investors have been placed according to the risk/reward projects they are normally interested in. This is a simplification since each group of investors consists of many individuals, but it gives a good indication of their preferences.

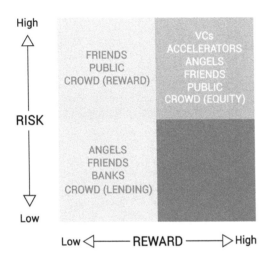

Venture capital. Venture capital funds are looking to invest in companies that can be resold for hundreds of millions of euros within a few years. They are looking for extremely high rewards but are also willing to take high risks. Only a very small fraction of startups qualify for this kind of reward, and one of the biggest mistakes in the funding process for startups is to spend your time chasing venture capital funds when you clearly don't have an interesting proposal for them.

Startup accelerators. Startup accelerators are looking for startups that can become very big, and are essentially looking for the same types of deals as venture capital funds.

Business angels. Most business angels are also looking for something that can become 'big', but they're not as extreme as venture capitalist funds in their requirements for return, so you don't have to approach them with something that could be worth hundreds of millions. Even if your startup isn't the next big thing, business angels might be interested anyway. One of the biggest mistakes founders make when approaching business angels is to believe business angels are only driven by financial return. Money is only one reason why business angels invest in startups.

Banks. Unlike other funding sources, banks don't provide equity but instead they lend money

 © 2017 Nicolaj Højer Nielsen

to companies in return for interest. They don't therefore gain anything amazing if your company suddenly becomes massively successful. With only a very low reward potential (interest rate), they are only willing to take very low risks. Many startups make the mistake of chasing bank loans when their startup clearly has way too much risk to be interesting to banks.

Crowdfunding. Crowdfunding attracts different investors depending on the crowdfunding model. With reward-based crowdfunding, individuals take a risk on unproven products because they feel some kind of affinity with the company; in exchange, they receive a discount or another non-financial reward. Equity crowdfunding attracts slightly higher investments in exchange for equity, with the risk of failure offset by potentially having shares in 'next big thing'. Crowdlending is a safer investment, where investors receive interest but play no part in the upside when a startup succeeds.

Friends/family. Friends and family don't really invest in your business – they invest in you. This also means they invest all over the place – even in projects that don't make sense from a financial point of view.

Public support. Many startup projects generate value for society, and governments all over the world want to provide financial support to startups in their various forms. A common mistake made by startups is to overlook this very important source of funding.

When do investors invest?

The funding sources are not only different in regards to WHAT they invest in, but also WHEN they want to provide funding for your company.

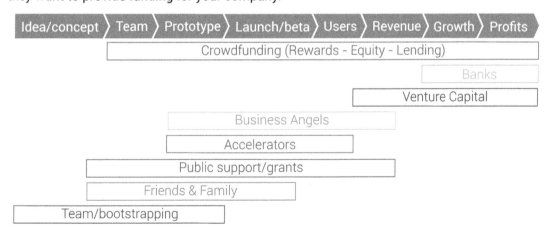

Crowdfunding. Reward crowdfunders normally invest quickly and for personal reasons, which means they'll invest earlier than most professional investors. But they need something to get excited about, so at least a semi-functional prototype is usually required. Equity crowdfunding normally attracts higher investments in the hope of a large financial reward, so success is more likely after the first professional funding rounds, while crowdlending is later again. Crowdlending platforms normally won't even accept a campaign unless the company has a stable cashflow.

Banks. Startup founders should forget about banks in the initial phases. The risk is simply too high for banks to be interested until the company is early-stage positive. But some public support programmes exist that can de-risk the projects in a bank's mindset and thereby make a bank loan more accessible earlier in the process.

Venture capital. Venture capital funds are willing to take very high risks in their pursuit of very high financial rewards. Many startup founders believe that a willingness to take risks means venture capital funds invest mainly when the startup is at the idea stage. Nothing could be further from the truth. A venture capital fund normally invests when there are signs of commercial traction, meaning the company has launched its first product and generates a lot of users and/or revenue.

Business angels. Business angels invest earlier than venture capital funds. But even business angels ideally want some traction before they invest. This doesn't need to be real revenue, but ideally means the company has already gathered a talented team which has built the first beta product.

Startup accelerators. These are willing to go in early because they see their role as accelerating startups to a point where they can get further financing – typically from business angels or venture capital funds. But even accelerators want more than a business idea. As a minimum they want to invest in a talented team which already has built a prototype of the intended product.

Public support programmes. There are public support programmes even from the very early phases, but the majority of those work only on a co-financing basis. This means that the government only pays part of the costs and the startup needs to find supplementary funding from other sources.

Friends and family. All professional investors want some traction before they'll be interested in investing. So which initial investors will provide you with money before the professionals step in? In many cases, your friends and family!

 Key note: You don't need to raise all your money now!

A common mistake among entrepreneurs is trying to raising ALL the money they need for their company – from the idea stage to the point where the company is profitable – on day one. This is almost always impossible since many investors, especially those with deeper pockets than you and your friends/family, won't invest until you've got more traction. So focus on raising enough for the next milestone which will attract different investors!

 © 2017 Nicolaj Højer Nielsen

Case study: Funding for The CloakRoom – different investors for different stages

The CloakRoom case illustrates that different types of investors are attracted to different development stages. The CloakRoom is a personal (online) shopping service that makes it easier for men to dress well

Co-founder Kasper Brandi Pedersen explains:

We initially got €20,000 from friends and then we started contacting business angels. The introductions we got through our network were to traditional tech investors, but they didn't like our labour-intensive and inventory-heavy concept, and therefore decided not to invest. The angel we eventually found, via LinkedIn, was a former entrepreneur from South Africa who had recently moved to Amsterdam.

He loved brainstorming with two hungry entrepreneurs. We asked him for advice several times, and at some point he proposed putting in €10,000.

When we were later about to accept a seed investment from a crappy fund, he thought it was a stupid move and decided to up his offer to €150,000. He turned out to be the greatest guy ever, extremely talented and helpful, always available, and always cutting through the bullshit. We learnt a lot from him and still do. Even though we are 250 people now, we still regularly ask for his advice.

INVESTMENT TYPE	FRIENDS & FAMILY	BUSINESS ANGEL	VENTURE CAPITAL (seed round)	EXISTING INVESTORS (bridge round)	ACQUIRED BY COMPETITOR
INVESTMENT SIZE	€20k	€150k	€1.2m	€1.5m	Equity deal
COMPANY AGE	0 years	0.5 years	1 year	2 years	2.5 years

We only started seed fundraising when the traction was very clear. The business case was easy to understand; we had huge customer demand and were struggling to ship enough boxes from our little showroom. We needed €1m to scale the operations and that's what we raised. It was a clear investment case and the fundraising went pretty smoothly. We actually accepted the first term sheet we received from Connect Ventures who turned out to be a great partner.

After the seed round we got almost unlimited scalability because we partnered with an external warehouse and made deals with 50 brands. Our growth was explosive and we had a lot of interest from VCs across Europe, from which we hoped to raise the first real VC round (Series A). We must have met with 15 VCs in London alone, but in the end we didn't manage to close a deal.

The lack of a deal was caused by a sudden slowdown in growth. Our growth had doubled every quarter, and our marketing team made some very nice projections for how many customers they could get via Facebook for an acceptable customer acquisition cost (CAC). But suddenly the pool of leads dried up – we had simply reached everyone we could reach on Facebook too many times so that the number of new customers quickly went down.

When you're on a roll as an entrepreneur you tend to think that growth will continue forever as long as you keep pushing and hacking, but there's always a wall. However, investors aren't excited about startups that have had little or no growth for three months, no matter how rapid the past growth was. It's just too risky and there are plenty of startups with consecutive growth to choose from.

We had to make a choice between slowing down growth and trimming the organisation, or accepting a bridge round from existing investors at a lower valuation. Since my co-founder and I still had a combined equity stake of 70 per cent, we chose existing investors for the down round (a down round is startup jargon for a financing round where the share price is now lower than the previous investment round).

The bridge round gave us enough financial wiggle space to stabilise growth and improve unit economics, however that is not a sexy mission for aggressive young entrepreneurs. We had no ambition to be a local champion. We wanted to keep growing, which required substantial investments in inventory and supply chain optimisation. Therefore, we started talking to a range of old-school retailers and e-commerce competitors.

The best offer came from a German competitor, Modomoto, who had built their own fulfilment centre from scratch instead of outsourcing. No one else in our niche had done that. Combined with their superior tech stack, this made their unit economics the best in the business. To make it even better, they were only active in German speaking countries, whereas we were the market leader in Denmark, Sweden, the Netherlands and Belgium. The business case was clear: by combining the operational efficiency and profitability of Modomoto with the customer satisfaction and high order value of The Cloakroom, we would be positioned for market leadership in all our seven markets.

 © 2017 Nicolaj Højer Nielsen

One month after we signed the papers I was living in Berlin working for the merged company. We integrated the two organisations on a technical level first, which turned out to be less painful than the cultural integration between the two offices. In January 2017, 12 months after the acquisition, we were able to run all functions from Berlin and it was time to close the Dutch office down. It was a beneficial financial decision, but a painful process. My co-founder and I decided to leave our positions and we now are financially safe because we hold equity in a big German company run by smart people, while we are free to build new startups. However it was hard to say goodbye to the greatest rollercoaster ride of our lives.

Do you really want their money? Now?

By now you know what kind of companies different types of investors are looking for and when in the process they are interested in investing. Knowing that will greatly increase your chances of conducting a successful fundraising campaign by approaching the right investors at the right time!

The question is, do you really want the investors' money?

Why shouldn't you? Well, first of all because no investor will be giving you the money for the sake of your blue eyes – except your mum and uncle, of course. The rest want something in return – a share of the company. In startup jargon this is called 'dilution', when your share of the company is diluted by investors.

The example below illustrates a typical dilution for a company that receives funding from the usual suspects at the different stages of the company. It starts with you getting a co-founder, and having friends, angels and accelerators invest in the company. Next you give shares to the first employee and later employees in the form of an option pool, and then you receive huge investment from a local venture capital fund and later an international venture capital fund.

So is going from 100% of a very small cake to 17% of (hopefully) a large cake worth it? This depends on your specific situation and what you really want to do with your startup. Is it more important for you to be in control of your company, even if it's a small one, than to grow it into a world-leading company? Then you certainly shouldn't go this route! But if you have a startup where you need funding to grow, or grow fast enough, VC and other types of investors might be exactly what you need!

You should ask yourself: *Do we really need the money? Will the money really make a tremendous difference for our company – or could we achieve what we want without it? And if we need money, do we need it now or could it wait till later?*

Splitting equity in your startup

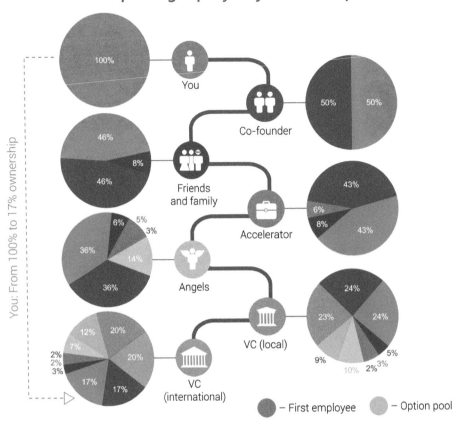

It's hard to find entrepreneurs who regret they didn't take in external investors earlier in the journey, while it's easy to find entrepreneurs who regret taking in investors too early when (they know with hindsight) they would have been able to bootstrap longer.

Why do they regret it? In many cases because they now know the huge value jumps a startup takes when reaching new milestones. Whereas the value of an idea is close to zero, the value skyrockets as the startup builds a team and prototype, launches a product, gets revenue and starts to grow rapidly. The value is exemplified below with the pre-money valuation of Recon Instruments during different stages.

 © 2017 Nicolaj Højer Nielsen

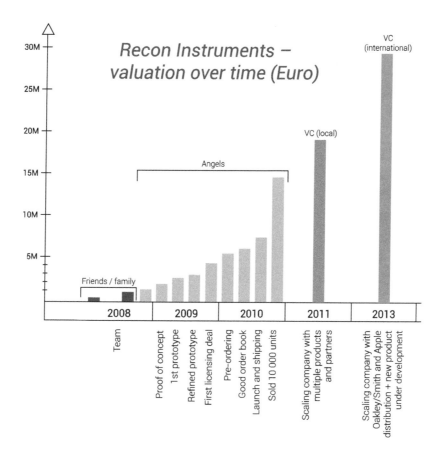

Recon Instruments – valuation over time (Euro)

Recon Instruments was a Vancouver-based startup, founded in 2007 and sold to Intel in 2015. The idea was to combine electronics with sports equipment in the form of swim goggles, snow goggles and sun glasses, with built-in head-up display (HUD).

The first investments you take in are very expensive since the value of your company is low. So you will have to give up a lot of your company to the investor for a relatively small amount of money if you take investors in early on. And if you end up taking too much money too early, you might end up owning only a small fraction of your company at exit. This not only impacts your financial upside but also your ability to be in control of your company.

Take-away points

Different types of investors have very different appetites for risk. What's attractive for one type of investor can be much less attractive to another simply because they invest in a different corner of the investor matrix. Those looking for high risk/high reward cases include venture capital funding, startup accelerators and business angels, while banks are looking for something completely different.

The risk/reward of an individual startup changes as it goes through the different phases. Typically, the first to invest in a startup are your friends and family because they invest in you and not your business. Most professional investors want to see more progress before they invest.

Even if you come to a point where you can get external funding, you should think twice before accepting the investment since it will involve you owning a smaller share of the company and also result in potentially loss of control of your company.

 © 2017 Nicolaj Højer Nielsen

© 2017 Nicolaj Højer Nielsen

——————— Chapter 4: ———————

Why can't you find
an investor?

As a first-time entrepreneur, you probably think your idea is cool, has huge value and investors will trip over themselves to give you their money. They won't. Your great idea is probably not great − and even if it is great, it's almost certainly not original.

Investors don't invest in ideas

Every first-time entrepreneur, including myself when I founded my first company, thinks coming up with the idea is the hardest part of the startup, and the part where the idea is put into practice is the easy part. Nothing could be further from the truth and that's the primary reason why your idea alone will not find funding.

When I was a graduate student at Copenhagen Business School, I had an idea for a business, an online magazine. This was 1999, so it was quite new at that time. My idea was for a magazine by amateurs that published their articles about cars, girls and gadgets; an online version of the magazines GQ and FHM.

I thought it worked like this: I'd make a business plan and send it to investors. The investors would then also think it was a great idea and they would give me the money I needed. With that money I could create my website, get customers, build a company and conquer the world. That is how I thought it would work. Really.

It didn't. I spent weeks writing a business plan and sent it to a lot of potential investors (venture capital funds) with no results. No one was interested in investing in my idea! Why?

Because no one invests in a business idea alone.

Today, 15 years later, I meet plenty of students and entrepreneurs who think just like I did then. What they think is a *brilliant* business idea is most likely not a brilliant business idea. And what they think is *just* implementation is not just implementation. An investor will start the discussions by reminding you that your idea is nothing. What happens afterwards is what creates value. A bad idea with brilliant execution is better than a brilliant idea with bad execution.

 © 2017 Nicolaj Højer Nielsen

Case study: Recon Instruments – an idea that wasn't unique

My friend Dan Eisenhardt co-founded the previously mentioned startup Recon Instruments in 2007. As a former competitive swimmer, he wanted information about how he was performing delivered to him in real time, in the form of goggles and glasses with built-in head-up display (HUD).

Was it a unique idea? Not really – even though I initially thought so.

I was one of the first investors. I helped Dan and his co-founders secure further funding and reached out to my network to look for potential investors. One of my former classmates, Rudi Airisto, responded and said he wanted to invest in the company. But the really interesting thing was the files Rudi attached to his email containing drawings of a product idea that was very close to the vision behind Recon Instruments.

What Dan and the rest of us thought might be a unique idea, wasn't. In my network alone, there was at least one person who had the same idea, and that meant it was likely that hundreds of people across the globe had thought of the exact same idea as Dan. Fast forward eight years; the company became a success and was sold to Intel in 2015. The success of Recon Instruments wasn't due to the founders having a

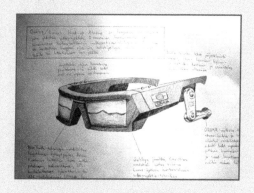

great idea at the right point in time. It was a success because the people *wanted* to do it, and they did the hard work necessary for the next eight years. They created a success not based on the idea but based on the execution with numerous small, smart decisions over a number of years.

Key note: Ideas are not worth much

Investors know that what separates a successful startup from a failure is not the unique idea but the hard work done by the team in the many years following the initial idea. And that's exactly why most investors don't invest in ideas.

What are investors looking for?

So if your idea isn't enough, what more are investors looking for? What kind of progress/traction do they want? Of course, all investors are different but their analysis can be summed up in the following three areas on which they evaluate the risk/reward profile of your startup:

MARKET

Market risk – Are there customers for your product? Who needs your product and will they choose it over alternative solutions?

TECH

Technical risk – Can it be made? Is it technically feasible to make the intended product? And can it be made at a cost which makes it competitive with alternatives?

TEAM

Team risk – Do you and your team have the necessary skills? Can you execute and bring this idea to the market better than competing teams? Are you good enough?

 © 2017 Nicolaj Højer Nielsen

Market risk

Many startups go under because there isn't a real demand for their products. Even if you, as founder, believe the product will solve a 'big problem' for many people, this may not apply to the real world. So the initial analysis by investors is often centred around the following questions: *Is there a real demand for the intended product, will enough people buy this product* and *how much will they be willing to pay for it?*

Examples of products where investors evaluate early-stage startups with low versus high risk:

LOW PERCEIVED MARKET RISK	HIGH PERCEIVED MARKET RISK
Pharmaceuticals	Diagnostics
E-commerce	Consumer apps/games
Consulting/professional services	B2B software

 Key note: Investors focus a lot on market risk!

Most startups believe the technical risk of making the product is the biggest problem, when what often kills startups is not a lack of a good product, but a lack of customers. For many innovators, the market risk is even higher than the product risk. You have invented a cool product but will people buy it? In your dialogue with investors you will have to focus on convincing them (ideally with real data) that there is an actual need for your product!

Of course, the level of market risk varies a lot from startup to startup. Some early-stage startups have a very high degree of market risk while others don't.

The archetype for a startup with high market risk could be a company that wants to develop applications (apps) for consumers. Yes, we have all heard about the success of Angry Birds – the mobile game which earns the company Rovio hundreds of millions of euros in revenue per year. But did you know that Rovio produced 51 unsuccessful mobile games before hitting the jackpot with Angry Birds? And Rovio isn't special in that sense. It is very hard to predict pre-launch if a mobile app will be successful or not, and therefore many of the world's most prestigious and successful game developers have statistics similar to Rovio's.

The same high market risk goes for most types of consumer software and apps. We have all heard about the handful of very successful apps most of us use such as Facebook, Instagram or Dropbox. But every day there are more than a thousand new apps launched. Every single day! How many become huge or successful enough to support a small company? Not many! So when entrepreneurs pitch 'I have this great idea for a new app', most investors are cynical and want to see real customer data before they'll be convinced this could really be the next big thing. Coming up with an idea for an app is rarely enough, but the good part is that you can usually develop a beta-version (a minimum viable product), on a limited budget (financed by yourself or by friends and family), and use this to show there's demand for your product. If you can do this, investors will stand in line to invest!

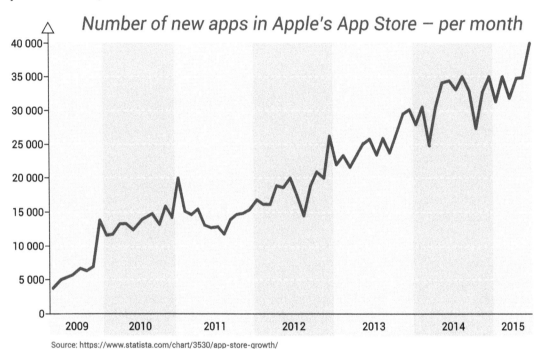

Number of new apps in Apple's App Store – per month

Source: https://www.statista.com/chart/3530/app-store-growth/

Technical risk

While there might be a market opportunity (demand for your intended product), technical challenges could prevent you from taking advantage of that opportunity. For example, there might be a demand for selling trips to the moon for €10,000 per person, but can it be done? Is the technology available to take people there and bring them back safely for a cost you can make money from?

 © 2017 Nicolaj Højer Nielsen

LOW PERCEIVED TECHNICAL RISK	HIGH PERCEIVED TECHNICAL RISK
Consumer apps/games	Pharmaceuticals
E-commerce	Cleantech
Most IT startups	University spinouts in general

Some startups have huge technical risks while others have low risks and this impacts how potential investors perceive the opportunity. Let's illustrate this with a startup that has a high degree of technical risk:

Researchers who want to make more efficient batteries

One very interesting research area with huge commercial potential is the improvement of current energy storage technologies (batteries). For years consumers have found it a major pain to have to recharge their mobile phones daily, but now this pain has spread into many other industries (car/home batteries, storage of electricity generated by wind turbines etc.). In all these industries there is a need for more efficient batteries as the world tries to move away from fossil fuels. Entrepreneurs and investors have of course spotted this 'billion-dollar' opportunity and are pouring money into tons of startups that are trying to make better forms of energy storage. But these startups also carry huge technical risks! It's a long and very bumpy road from showing potential in the laboratory to actually making it commercially available to consumers and businesses worldwide. Are you able to replicate the positive results? Are you able to produce it on a huge scale? Will the technology be stable and safe enough to implement outside the lab in houses/factories? Are you able to produce the batteries at a cost so low that it will be commercially attractive? There's a huge technical risk but the business opportunity is so enormous that investors are willing to take that risk.

Other startups have much lower risk of failing due to technical issues. A good example of startups could be within e-commerce. Most likely you are using existing software for your online shop that you have purchased from third parties and adjust to your needs (design, integration with other IT systems). It will cost you money and time to implement, but there is very little risk that it can't be done. In this case investors aren't concerned about technical risks.

Whether or not you suffer from market or technical risk, most investors realise you suffer from at least one risk – the risk of your team not executing the plan.

Team risk

This is the risk that is you; the risk of you and your team not having the skills or experience required to take full advantage of a given market opportunity.

Even with startups that have high market risk and/or high technology risk, the team risk is seen by many investors as the biggest risk factor associated with startups. It doesn't matter if the market opportunity is huge and the technology is available for making the product. If you and your team don't have the required skills to execute it successfully, you will fail in the development or sales phase, or be beaten by the competition who will take advantage of the market opportunity better and faster than you.

(!) Key note: Can YOU really do it?

Many startups fail to raise money from investors, not because they can't communicate the huge business opportunity, but because they fail to convince the investors that *they* – the team – can take full commercial advantage of it.

The contrary is also possible. I know of investors who have funded a startup *without* being convinced about the market opportunity and knowing there is high technical risk. Why? Because they saw a strong team with the stamina and drive needed to face and overcome the market and technical challenges they will meet.

A good example of how a great team can impress investors is Airbnb. Paul Graham from Y Combinator didn't really believe in the Airbnb business model, but he saw a great team that had managed to survive a year without investor funding by selling cereals. He believed if they could sell cereals they could sell anything and they could make Airbnb a success.

Why are investors so focused on a strong team and less on your business idea? Because your idea is really only an untested hypothesis about the world. You have defined a problem that some people or companies have, and you have come up with a solution to that problem. But is that actually true?

One of the most interesting studies on what makes startups succeed or fail, is the Startup Genome project. Based on data from 3,200 technology startups, the team of researchers from Startup Genome investigated whether sticking to the startup's initial business idea or changing strategy along the way impacted the chance of success.

Startup Genome concluded that startups that change a major part of their business once or twice are more successful than startups that change strategy more than twice or not at all.

In other words, your initial assumptions are most likely wrong and you will have to adapt as you learn more about your customers and their demands. The chances that your original idea is polished enough to create a successful company is very slim.

All investors know that, and that is why they won't be impressed by your 'great' idea alone.

 © 2017 Nicolaj Højer Nielsen

They want a team that is so strong they will convert the 'bad' Plan A, to a successful Plan B or C.

Case study: Bootstrapping at AirHelp

Background: AirHelp is a startup that helps travellers get compensation when flights are delayed, cancelled or overbooked. Air-Help does the paperwork, follow-up and legal action, in return for 25% of the compensation amount awarded from successful claims.

Henrik Zillmer, CEO and founder of AirHelp, gives his view on funding:

Don't start with fundraising!

This is the biggest mistake you can make as an entrepreneur. Unless you've started a lot of companies in the past with a couple of successful exits, you're not able to raise capital without showing traction first.

During the first year of a startup, you need to spend all your time validating your business model and getting traction. When you have a beautiful hockey stick curve to show, you're ready to fundraise. Any time sooner and you'll end up wasting your time and, more seriously, spend less time on actually building your company.

Imagine being the investor. Ask yourself: Would you invest in a startup with an idea, but no traction, or would you invest in one that shows an increasing customer base, retention and revenue?

"But I can't afford a year without salary," you say.

Of course you can! Ask your bank or your friends for a loan. If you're not willing to make sacrifices, entrepreneurship isn't for you. Reducing your standard of living for a time is only the beginning.

That's how we started in AirHelp. We bootstrapped for 12 months, living from savings and credit card debt and then, only after we reached a steady flow of new customers, did we move into fundraising mode.

Take-away points

Entrepreneurs must start to think like investors if they are to be successful in securing funding for their startup project. This means thinking and working in terms of *technical risk*, *market risk* and *team risk*.

When you start up your project, all three types of risk are high since you haven't proved anything yet. The chances of getting an investor to invest when you are at the idea stage is therefore very low! The more an entrepreneur can reduce these three risks, the more attractive the project becomes to investors in general and less equity needs to be 'paid' for the investment.

The first step in reducing the risk - and improving the perceived reward – of your startup is to gather a strong team around you. Investors know it's the team, and their skills and hard work over several years that make a startup successful, not the initial idea. Your team and your co-founders are therefore your first investors, and they are the topic of the next chapter.

 © 2017 Nicolaj Højer Nielsen

Chapter 5

Co-founders are your first investors

You de-risk your business idea by working on the project via your own funds – bootstrapping – until it reaches a point where its risk/reward is attractive to investors. The first and most important bootstrapping step is getting co-founders on board and getting the right team in place. You will most likely not be able to pay co-founders properly and they are therefore your first investors. They invest their time but not money and are crucial for attracting investors later.

Why have co-founders?

Do I really need co-founders this early on? The answer is 'yes' and here is why:

1. Co-founders add competencies

If you're good at building a product, chances are you're not the world's greatest salesperson – and vice versa. Your startup project needs both, and if there's only you then you are going to fail. You are working to prove that your business is viable and that investors should therefore invest. In most cases this work involves both building the first version/prototype of your product (to reduce technical risk) and getting the first users/customers/partners on board (to reduce market risk). You need co-founders who complement your core competencies to achieve initial traction.

2. Co-founders add credibility

Even if you're the type of person who can cover all the bases yourself, it won't do you much good in relation to investors. Investors believe and invest in the team. Remember, you don't build the team simply to secure funding but also to build the longer-term business. If it is only you, chances are investors will say 'no'.

It is very unlikely that all the distinct skills needed to drive forward a startup are within the same person. Even if I meet one person I believe has all these skills (and I haven't yet), I will

 © 2017 Nicolaj Højer Nielsen

wonder what will happen if they're run over by a car tomorrow. I will also be concerned this is a one-man band because they've been unable to convince anyone else to join their company. Is something wrong? Don't they want anyone else in or does no one want to join because of them? Either way, it's a red flag in the eyes of most professional investors.

Advice from an investor: Never invest in one-person startups!

Lars Buch was in charge of Startupboot-camp in Copenhagen for three years before turning to a corporate venture at Leo Innovation Lab. Here Lars explains his view on founding teams:

Normally I wouldn't invest in a single founder (or in a team where one person owns the shares and the team have no ownership), because being a single founder normally means one of three things: it's too early to invest, the founder underestimates what's needed to build something sustainable, or the founder is simply an asshole.

I'm OK starting a dialogue with a very strong, single founder, but then the very first (only) topic will be about what critical resources are needed to build this company, and there will be no actual transfer of money before those resources are in place.

Which co-founders do you need?

One of the most extensive studies into what makes startups successful was done by the researchers at Startup Genome. Data from thousands of (mainly IT) startups was processed in order to determine the common factors that successful startups share. One of the most important findings was that startups which have a balanced team of both a technical founder and a business founder are far more successful in the long term, compared with startups that have either a technical or a business founder.

Balanced founder teams raised on average 30% more money, grew the customer base by 290% more, and were less likely to fail when compared with non-balanced teams.

These findings match the experiences of most investors with regards to the set of core team competencies they need to see – product development and sales.

Product development

You need someone who can develop the product. The type and kind of developer you need obviously depends on the specifics of your project. Without such a co-founder (if you don't have the technical skills yourself), it will be hard both to bootstrap the startup and to convince investors to come in.

A typical example is that of a business-oriented entrepreneur who has an idea for an app but doesn't have someone with the technical skills needed on board. The entrepreneur is essentially in the process of building a software company without a software developer on the team. Investors will take one look at this and turn away.

"If you're starting a restaurant and you can't cook, you need to team up with a chef."

 Key note: Help! I can't find a technical co-founder

Finding the right person to fill the position of technical co-founder can be difficult. I often come across startups looking for a developer who wants to become a co-founder but can't convince anyone to join. There are several reasons for this: good developers are in short supply, and many of those who could consider joining have worked with people who have promised them a lot but delivered very little. A third reason is that developers tend to not be risk takers. Many of them aren't entrepreneur material.

For these three reasons you have a lot of business people chasing a few potential technical co-founders and promising them riches. After they have been promised this one or two times they become immune to offers.

If you're struggling to find a technical co-founder, you should consider outsourcing to show that you, as a business person, are committed to the business and attempting to get some traction. Get an agency to develop the first version of the app, even if the result is much simpler than your grand vision. Do a beta launch and hopefully you will have positive feedback from the first users. Now you have something to show and this will make it easier to convince a technical co-founder (and later investors) to join.

 © 2017 Nicolaj Højer Nielsen

Sales

You also need a dedicated salesperson to join your founding team – an extrovert who likes to communicate with the outside world, with customers, partners, vendors and investors. Someone who is good at selling the project and the vision. In startup jargon, they're sometimes called a 'product visionary'.

These sales are not only to customers but to all key stakeholders, and that's why it's a full-time job, even if your company's product has not yet been fully developed.

Think about the differences in competencies needed in small versus large organisations. If you're working in a big company, all your competencies are there in the organisation and the majority of your stakeholders are internal. If you need a product manager, legal advice or a marketing graphic drawn, all the competencies are found inside the organisation. You still need to convince the other employees to help you realise your goal, but you're all in the same boat and that tends to make things easier.

Working in small vs. large companies

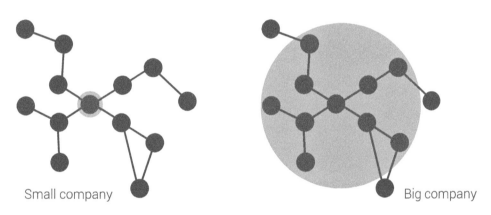

Small company   Big company

In a small startup the internal bubble is much smaller: you and your co-founder(s). When you need funding you need external investors; when you need marketing you need to collaborate with an external marketing company. Every time you need something extra you need to look outside the organisation. Basically, all the important resources are controlled by external stakeholders and you can't call your boss to have them do as you like. You need to convince them, and in many cases you need to convince them in other ways than paying them huge bucks now (since you're bootstrapped, your finances are most likely limited). You need to sell your project and vision to them and make them want to work with you rather than taking a better-paid position elsewhere. This 'sales job' quickly turns into a more than full-time dedicated position.

Key note: You need the salesperson now

You need the sales guy from day one to build all the external relationships – you can't wait until your product is developed and needs to be launched. That's too late! Investors know that, and generally prefer teams with technical and sales resources present when they invest.

Could you use outsourcing or regular employees instead?

The purpose of bootstrapping is to bring the company sufficiently forward to make it fundable in the eyes of investors. But you could argue that getting a co-founder on board is just one means of bringing the company forward, so let's discuss two obvious alternatives to getting a co-founder:

1. Outsourcing, where you pay an external company by the hour or per project
2. A formal employee on a long-term contract

Using outsourcing

I sometimes hear from business entrepreneurs who say, 'Well I can sell, I can do marketing, I can do PR but I can't code, so I found this software development company who can develop the app for me'. And I hear technical developers say, 'We are the software guys, we invented this software. We can't sell, but we have found a sales/marketing agency that will do the selling for us'.

Both are typical examples of outsourcing where you try to outsource either the development or the commercialising to external parties. In theory this sounds good: you stick to what you're good at, keep a hundred per cent of the equity of the company, and hire external companies to do the rest. In practice it hardly ever works like this.

The first obvious problem is whether you can afford to pay the outsourcing company for their assistance. They bill you like any other client and that can quickly become very expensive. Startup projects tend to take much longer to be successful due to longer development times and because getting the first customers on board takes time.

The other reason why early-stage outsourcing rarely works is that the task is still in progress. You might have decided that your app should feature functions a, b, c, d and e, but shortly after the first customers have tried the app, you realise you need functions f, g and h. A lot of startup work is based on assumptions and with every step forward you learn some of your assumptions are wrong. This is how it goes for most app-based startups. In fact, this is the nature of starting up. Mistakes need to be made to arrive at the final successful product.

⚠ Key note: Outsourcing scares away investors!

It is very hard to get outsourced core competencies to work in the early days of your company, and even if you believe you can, it often scares away potential investors because they themselves have had a bad experience with it.

You need both business and technical people who are in from the outset and committed to going the full distance. And that is the problem with outsourcing: the people you outsource to aren't committed to your project in the same way as you. Say, for example, you get the first version of the app back from them and you quickly realise changes need to be made. You will have to pay them each time because they are not invested in the project the way you are and don't work for free. They bill you by the hour or job. Co-founders don't think like that. They think long-term and in terms of building a successful company. That is what investors want to see, and why they will say 'no' to startups where either sales or research and development (R&D) has been outsourced.

What a VC looks for in a startup team

Ulla Brockenhuus-Schack, General Partner at SEED Capital, explains:

It's extremely demanding to build a company and only the strongest and most dynamic teams survive. It is therefore crucial your team has diverse competences. That means you have a product visionary: someone with industry expertise, capable of building relationships and selling your vision to clients and investors; and you have a tech rock star: a product developer who can implement that vision and attract further tech talent. These are core institutional skills, which need to be deeply embedded in the company, and not something you buy.

Outsourcing key functions doesn't work as startups depend on being agile. Also, making up for the skills your team doesn't have by outsourcing important tasks is expensive, and will give you less time to prove your worth before you run out of money.

Exceptions to the rule – use outsourcing as a short-term solution.

Outsourcing some key skills can work in the initial phases of the startup because creating a team is sometimes a catch-22; you are trying to convince team members to join this fantastic new company but you don't have any track history. So you could get a prototype made by an external outsourcing agency to test the market assumptions and use it to attract the potential developer who will become the co-founder. Or you outsource the sales side and hire a part-time business developer to test market assumptions and get some letters of intent or generate interest, then you can use this success to get the co-founder salesperson involved. So, long-term outsourcing doesn't work but you can use outsourcing in the short-term to get started on testing your assumptions and to attract the talented co-founders you really want.

The contrarian view: I don't need a software developer in the founding team!

For 99 per cent of professional investors, having no developer is a deal breaker when looking at a software startup to invest. But there are some for whom this is not the case, in most cases because they themselves have succeeded using outsourcing in the initial stage of the development phases.

Thor Angelo has successfully used IT outsourcing for several startups he has started or invested in. He explains his thoughts on what it takes:

Not having a software developer on my team is not a deal breaker. Of course having one will not hurt, but I know you can get it to work without one. For me it's more important to have the product visionary on the core team where the initial software development can be outsourced.

That's why in all the projects where I'm founder or investor, I have the initial develop-

 © 2017 Nicolaj Højer Nielsen

ment tasks outsourced to the Ukraine. I've found a good outsourcing company there which I use to get the 'minimum viable product' developed. Later in the process we can move the development closer to the rest of the team by building up an internal development team.

I believe that one of the 'secrets' in making such outsourcing work is a short cultural distance. For European startups that will mean using teams in Eastern Europe (Lithuania, Ukraine, Poland etc.) and not further away such as China and India. A too-large cultural distance makes collaboration way too hard!

Another common mistake made by startups when outsourcing is not having properly specified the development tasks up front. This involves producing very detailed feature lists and mock-ups and agreeing a fixed price for such development. This is of course easier said than done since it requires you – the startup – to think and to test the detailed functionality of the mock-up with potential users before development starts. Many skip this point, which leads to a variety of problems when the development process starts and it turns out that the detailed functionality hasn't been agreed upon.

It definitely helps in the process if you have some technical understanding. This makes it much easier for you to specify the intended functionality in detail and also to discuss issues with the outsourcing company along the way. So if you lack technical understanding, team up with someone from your network to help you do the specifications and ask the development teams any technical questions.

Or to sum up: having no technical co-founder shouldn't be an excuse for you not to start your startup. You can certainly start by using an outsourcing company!

Employees not co-founders?

Outsourcing development or sales is a bad idea because the nature of the transaction is such that the resources focus on short-term gains and not the longer-term company vision. Could you hire people on regular contracts instead of making them co-founders of the company?

To clarify, a 'co-founder' is a person who has a significant equity stake in the company which they get in return for no, or a very low, initial salary. In contract terms, an 'employee' is a resource where the main motivation comes from the monthly salary and not from the long-term equity upside.

The first question is whether you can afford to hire an employee on a regular contract. Let's assume you want to start a software company and need a seasoned software developer to lead the product's development. The going rate for a skilled software developer in Western Europe can easily be €75,000 a year. And if they're just an employee and not co-founder, why should they work for you in a high-risk, early-stage startup instead of a secure, well-paid job in a big organisation or in another startup where they can become co-founder?

Even if you can afford to hire someone, you need to think twice. The benefit of hiring talent is that you don't have to give them a share of the company, but if they're thinking like a regular employee, they'll be unlikely to go the extra mile or stay with the company when things get tough. And things will get tough. Let's assume that your startup follows the path of most startups, where the first product doesn't sell very well. The salesperson you hired won't get a commission and will probably start looking for another company where they can earn that commission.

Again, co-founders don't think like that and that's why investors will tell you that's what you need – both on the sales and the technical side of the business. A co-founder will increase your chances of funding and long-term success.

 Key note: The beer test

How do I pick the right co-founder? Apart from their formal qualifications, ask yourself if you could drink a beer with that person. You are starting on a five or 10-year journey and you will spend more time with them than your wife or husband, so you need to find someone with the same vision for the future.

A lot of it is down to gut feeling. Do you want to drink beer with them? Do you want to be in the same room as them for the next five to 10 years, for more than 10 hours a day? If you aren't certain about having a beer with them, don't pick them. It's better to compromise a bit on formal qualifications and find someone you can work with. They can always improve their qualifications and skills, but if you can't get on with them, that's much more difficult to change.

Incentivising co-founders and early employees

You need co-founders who are driven by the long-term vision they're building. To ensure their loyalty, you need to provide them with equity.

But how much do you give away and to what types of team members? Below is an overview of the major differences between co-founders and early employees:

 © 2017 Nicolaj Højer Nielsen

	CO-FOUNDERS	EARLY EMPLOYEES
Joining the company when?	In the earliest days of the company – typically before launch and before external funding.	Typically joins company after the company has received funding and/or launched product
Company size	2 to approximately 4-5	4 upwards
Salary?	Initially often no salary, since company is bootstrapped. Later salary, but significantly below market rate.	Yes, but below market rate
Primary motivation for joining	Vision and equity stake	Mixed – both salary but also vision/equity
Typical equity stake	Initial equity to be shared either evenly among co-founders (typically 25-50%) or if main co-founder, the other minimum 10% equity.	Depends on both seniority and how early they get in. Very rarely more than 5% (and then only for exceptional hires or an experienced CEO) – typically much less.

How much equity should you give your co-founder?

Co-founders come in when there's no funding, no revenue, and therefore no money for a salary. But how much equity should they get in return for working for free and taking that risk?

Let's say you've spent time and money working on an idea. Six months later you bring in a co-founder – that could be a sales/marketing guy if you have the product development competencies. That person is willing to work for zero pay, and you both believe that realistically you are 12 months away from being able to pay yourselves a salary. The question is *how big a part of the pie should that co-founder get?*

0 100m   42km

My personal view: You have run 100 metres out of a marathon

One valid point of view is that you are the 'real' founder – you have come up with the idea, and have already spent a considerable amount of time and money developing it. So you should have much more equity than your co-founder who joins now. You might give that person an offer of 20 per cent of the equity and keep 80 per cent for yourself.

The other perspective is very different. Even though you've spent six months on the idea, it will most likely be 10 years before you have built a successful company. The steps you have taken so far are few compared to the steps you will take together for the next nine years. Ninety-five per cent of the work is still ahead of you. In this scenario, you would offer your co-founder a 50/50 deal because the real work is just getting started.

My personal view is more in line with the second perspective. You have just started on a long journey, you will be in the same boat together for many years, and you will need to make sure they are in it for the long run. I believe this is in your own interests, even though it will leave you with a smaller part of the cake – but now there's a much bigger chance the cake will be larger in the future!

An alternative scenario is a negotiation with the co-founder resulting in a quarter of your equity. Perhaps this satisfies the person for now, but what about in three or four years' time, after their share has been diluted by investors and stock options to employees?

· ·

 ### Key note: Too little equity for co-founders can disturb future investors

The uneven split among co-founders can also be a deal-breaker when negotiating with future investors. If a key person (as your co-founder by definition is) doesn't have a fair share of the equity, this will be perceived as a problem. They know that this might demotivate them later when they suddenly only have (say) five percent of the equity due to dilution.

The right number of co-founders is typically two to four. Or as the famous quote from Jeff Bezos, founder of Amazon, goes: *If you can't feed a team with two pizzas, it's too large.*

· ·

 © 2017 Nicolaj Højer Nielsen

Advice from an entrepreneur: Three co-founders is the magic number

Amir Schlachet is the co-founder and CEO of Global-e, a startup that provides online retailers in Europe and the US with a cost-effective and risk-free service that handles the complexities of their cross-border sales.

Here Schlachet shares his view on the optimal number of co-founders for a startup:

I believe a team of three equal-stake co-founders is the optimal structure for a startup founding team.

I have no idea how single founders can ever achieve anything without being super-men and/or having truckloads of luck. In today's highly complicated and fast-changing world, it's super-important to have multiple view points from people who are equally committed to the business, especially when important strategic decisions are made (and in a startup almost every decision can potentially be strategic for the business).

Two co-founders are better, but assuming they will have different viewpoints (which they should) on many topics, making decisions will not be easy, and may lead to unnecessary compromises or one side feeling like he's constantly overruled.

Four co-founders is a "crowd", leading to problems ranging from decision making (see the above rationale for two co-founders, only doubled), through to the founding team splitting into two "parties" of two co-founders each, holding opposing views. I actually know such a case, where the main VC investor told them only one couple could stay and the other one must be bought out. On top of that, each of the four co-founders has only a 25% stake in the company, which is quickly eroded in the first couple of rounds, potentially to the level where the stake of each co-founder is no longer meaningful enough for him/her to invest the time, money and effort necessary for the endeavour to succeed.

Taking the above into account, I believe a team of three is the magic number for a founding team. It provides the necessary level of viewpoint diversity, while making majority-vote decision making very easy, and allowing each founder to retain a sufficiently high stake in the company

Case study: Building a great team with no money

Instead of having your network as financial investors, you can have them invest time/work in return for equity in your company; as Peecho did.

Peecho is a Dutch online print-on-demand service that was started in 2009 by two ex-employees of Album-printer, Martjin Groot and Sander Nagtegaal. Peecho is a platform that connects websites to print facilities all over the world and offers a way for owners of digital content [websites] to monetise their content or audience because they can sell their digital content items in print to their visitors.

Initially, like most small startups, Peecho had trouble making ends meet and was searching for a way to get the company up and running despite a lack of capital. Founder Sander Nagtegaal explains how they did it by creating a community:

Obviously we didn't have any money – and I mean nothing; just enough to start the company, basically. First we needed a team, and we needed a good team because if you want to build a serious platform, you'll need awesome programmers. But such a team usually requires money so we planned on making a community that would work a fixed eight hours per week. This community as a whole would be entitled to a certain amount of stock [in the company], however, the community itself would decide how big the community was going to be, which was the catch. So we asked the best programmer we knew, 'Do you want to join? You are going to be the first member of the community and for now – you are the community. So if you want to add more people to the community, you're welcome, but then you'll have to share your equity.'

We gave him a chunk of the company and within four weeks we had four new programmers in the community working on it because the amount of work was simply too much for one person.

By creating a community and letting the lead programmer find and decide whom he wanted to work with, Peecho circumvented the trouble of finding and convincing skilled programmers to join, since the lead programmer only picked the best people he knew because he had to share his pull of shares. This approach enabled Peecho to find the right programmers to build a technical team and the initial four programmers are still working for the company today.

 © 2017 Nicolaj Højer Nielsen

What if...

Value is created *not* by the initial idea you (and perhaps your co-founders) had, but by the work done in the decade after. And because you often initially can't pay a decent salary to your early employees, you will have to give them shares in the company instead.

- -

(!) **Key note: Get the paperwork in place – including shareholders' agreements**

Entrepreneurs want to save money (which is great) and hate bureaucracy (which is also great). This often leads to a big problem: you don't get your paperwork in place with your co-founders! This creates problems in the future if/when a co-founder needs to leave the company (either in a good way or is forced out). Then you really miss the shareholders' agreement that regulates what happens in such a situation. Therefore, before you get funding – before your company is worth anything – you and your co-founders need to sit down with an experienced lawyer and get the paperwork for your startup in place. You will regret it many times over if you don't do this, and it *can't* wait until 'later'.

- -

But what if co-founders or early employees leave the company? Statistically, some will – for several reasons. Maybe they don't believe in the company's vision any more, or maybe a co-founder or early employee isn't performing and you want them to leave. A common mistake is to not include a take-back clause in the initial equity agreement that covers the event that a co-founder or early employee leaves the company.

So-called 'dead equity' shares in your company that are owned by persons not active in it can become a burden. They tend to demotivate active employees/co-founders: *Why should I work full-time for below market rate, and create value for the co-founders doing nothing just sitting outside the company with a lot of equity?* Investors know that and too much dead equity can become a deal breaker when you're looking for external funding.

This can be avoided by creating:

1. Rights to buy back the shares if the person leaves. This is typically used in cases where the co-founders have already divided up equity in the company among themselves. If the person isn't active anymore, the remaining parties will have the right to buy back the stock at a share price set way below market rate to make it unattractive to leave the company. You normally make a time period for the clauses, so after the co-founder has 'earned' their shares, the buyback right kicks in. This period is typically three or four years.

② Stock options where promised equity is earned over time. An option is the right to buy shares at a given time in the future at a predetermined price (typically very low). This instrument is typically used when hiring early employees to whom you want to give equity. Instead of getting equity up front, they earn it over time. And such a stock option program lasts typically three or four years in which a proportion of the shares are earned on a monthly basis. If the employee leaves after (say) six months, the company has only a very small equity at stake. Depending on the legal regulations (which differ from country to country), the company might even implement rights to buy back shares from the employees, even if these have already been vested and bought.

By doing the above, you can minimise the risk of having too much dead equity in your company!

Advice from a former VC: Avoid dead equity

Christian Thaler-Wolski is a former venture capitalist who now acts as mentor and advisor for startups. He strongly warns founders against dead equity:

By dead equity I mean shares in your startup that are not owned by persons actively contributing to the company. Dead equity is a big issue. In short, any shareholder in an early-stage startup that has neither invested real money, nor contributes actively, can be considered dead equity. We are not talking about one or two per cent for an advisor; we are talking 10, 20 or 30 per cent for a co-founder who has left, an angel who didn't invest real money, or a parent company that has equity simply because once upon a time it felt entitled.

Equity is the most expensive form of capital. There is NOTHING more valuable, because it's equity that's needed to ensure the long-term motivation of founders, key employees, board members and advisors in the many years it will take before the company becomes successful. Problems are easily created if the equity is spread too thinly because significant shares in the company are held by people who provide no value to the company. Therefore it is of the utmost importance that when founders start they have an agreement that stipulates vesting of shares and outlines what happens when one of them leaves prematurely.

 © 2017 Nicolaj Højer Nielsen

Key note: Use a good lawyer!

Never give equity to co-founders or early employees without having vesting or buy-back rights in place. Since the legal framework is relatively complex, and different from country to country, you need to get advice from a lawyer experienced in dealing with startup equity in your jurisdiction.

Take-away points

A strong team not only helps you build a great startup, it also helps attract outside funding in the future. Find a strong, complementary group of co-founders and early employees, and bootstrap your business to reduce the risk for investors. A good team requires (at the minimum) the core competencies of product development and sales.

These core competences shouldn't be outsourced. If you need to develop a product quickly, you can outsource some development work, but only for prototyping – this is the exception to the no outsourcing rule. Your core team should never be outsourced.

Typical mistakes when bootstrapping include not giving equity to your early employees, giving equity but no rights to take back that equity, and not getting good, local, country-specific legal advice.

Chapter 6:

Friends and family financing

What can you do when you realise that even with a great team on board, none of the professional investors think your project is interesting or mature enough, and you're running out of cash so bootstrapping isn't an option anymore? My bet is that you'll do what most other entrepreneurs do in that situation: turn to your friends and family for financing.

When friends and family invest in startups it is sometimes referred to as the "three Fs investing": friends, family and fools. Friends and family are often the first investors in a startup, and they are usually the least qualified to make decisions on the inherent risk and reward. They are the first of all non-professional investors and they make their investing decision because they know you and trust you – not because of your business idea or acumen.

To avoid becoming the fool, or risk taking advantage of friends and family and ruining relationships forever, read this chapter carefully.

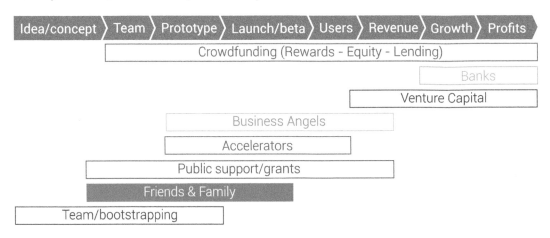

Case: Funding from friends and family – the Peecho story

Peecho is the previously mentioned print-on-demand platform for magazines and books.

The company got its initial traction via bootstrapping, but eventually needed additional funding. After failing to raise venture capital funding, Peecho decided talking to venture firms wasn't leading anywhere. They decided to try a completely different approach: raising the money from their friends and networks.

Sander Nagtegaal from Peecho explains: We made a list of people we knew; old bosses, people who were

 © 2017 Nicolaj Højer Nielsen

well known in the startup scene, successful entrepreneurs we knew etc. We made the list and said: 'Are they useful, can they spend some money and do we like them?' Then we filtered them, mainly on the 'do-we-like-them' question, and started calling them from the top. We said: 'We only have a product – we have no customers, no revenue. We are going to sell part of our shares right now and we have chosen you as one of the selected few. You can now buy one per cent of the company for €10,000. It's your call, no questions asked – take it or leave it!'

Within 20 minutes, Peecho had sold 10% of the company (€100.000) and had successfully got their first funding round. As Sander explains:

We should have done that two months before. Actually, I will never talk to VCs again at that stage of the company for money. I will talk to them for advice and customers. What they do is to talk to every company around, so they know everybody and can connect you to potential customers (B2B) – and usually they want to do that, especially if it's a portfolio company (of the VC) because then they can keep an eye on you. So if you are really successful with the customers of their portfolio companies they might move in because they have access to actual figures and data which is interesting to them.

Where do most startups get funding?

Despite what most entrepreneurs believe, investment from family and friends is one of the largest sources of capital for startups. Take a look at the image below. It shows where the money for funding startups actually comes from.

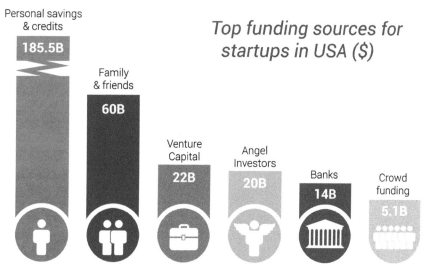

Source: https://www.fundable.com/learn/resources/guides/startup-guide/funding-your-startup

According to data compiled by Fundable, approximately 1% of startups are funded by angel investors and a tiny 0.05% is funded by VCs. Most startups (57%) are funded by personal savings and credit. The second largest source of funding (38%) is friends and family.

That's $60 billion that friends and family invest in startups in the US per year, more than the combined investments by VCs, business angels and banks. In other words, apart from your personal savings, friends and family are the biggest sources of capital for startups!

That fact is interesting because it is obscured by all the attention VCs and business angels get. You can't open a book or a newspaper without reading about a VC-funded startup, new angel investors or a crowdfunding success story. But behind all those headlines hides the fact that, after your own money, friends and family are the biggest sources of capital.

Case: LanguageWire – how a family member provided 'smart money'

LanguageWire was founded in 2000 and is now one of the top translation companies worldwide, with offices across Europe, €20 million in revenue and a hundred employees.

Co-founder of LanguageWire, Thor Anglo, explains how the founders got their first investor:

We had no clue about how and where to get funding for our startup when we started LanguageWire, so we wasted a lot of time contacting and meeting venture capital funds. These meetings gave us absolutely nothing and were very disappointing. The local VC funds were themselves very young and inexperienced at that time, and they didn't even seem to know we didn't have a case relevant to them.

We also went into dialogue with a public fund which actually offered us a rather bad deal which at the last minute we decided not to sign after advice from another entrepreneur. But there were not that many other potential investors – at least no one we knew of. How to get funding for a startup was like a black-box to us.

We ended up having a family member invest in our company and act as our 'business angel'. His initial investment was €150,000, followed by a further €150,000 if we reached some agreed milestones. In return he received 25 per cent of the shares in the company.

 © 2017 Nicolaj Højer Nielsen

He wasn't an experienced business angel, but he was a very experienced entrepreneur. He was an enormous help to us (especially in the first three or four years), providing us with a lot of practical advice on how to run a business. So for us this was for sure 'smart money' despite the fact he wasn't a formal business angel but a family member.

When do friends and family invest?

Friends and family invest right from the idea stage and continue investing almost up to the growth stage of a startup; they don't continue investing all the way to the end of the timeline when the amounts have become very big. That €10,000 from your uncle makes a hell of a difference when you're starting your business, but when you're growing your business from 10 employees and want to expand all over Europe you need €5 million. And most importantly – you are now in position to go to professional investors with much deeper pockets who are in the business of taking risks.

Why do friends and family invest?

Friends and family are non-professional investors because they invest in you, not your startup business venture. They invest because they like you, they trust you, and they know you. Of course, your friends and family will try to understand the business idea and they won't just write a blank cheque, but the overriding reason they invest is because of you – which is why they're willing to invest early. It's not because you've come up with a fantastic new concept; it's because they know you and want to support you even though what you're doing doesn't make that much sense to them.

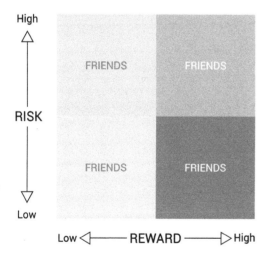

Because it's all about you and their relationship with you, friends and family invest in everything. This is unlike other types of investors or funding sources who have a clear position: the

VC who wants high risk/high reward or a bank that doesn't take risks. Friends and family are typically not risk averse – and they're not especially interested in or focused on any particular industry or technology.

Their desire to invest is dependent on your relationship with them, and they therefore invest in all quadrants of the risk/reward matrix, even in cases that, from a strict financial point of view, might not make sense.

Case study: Bidstack – 'anti-selling' to friends and family

James Draper is the founder and CEO of Bidstack, an online marketplace that enables anyone to bid on unsold, last-minute, digital billboard space to promote their message for minutes or hours. He explains his experience of raising money from friends and his personal network:

I had basically nothing but an idea – no name, contracts/contacts etc. – but I needed some money to start realising the grand vision of the company. I therefore started to reach out to my extended network for some initial funding.

When raising money in the extended friends and family round, we were careful to take money from people who could afford to lose it. Many got over-excited by the Bidstack concept, but were going to overstretch themselves financially.

I spent just as much time anti-pitching the concept to them as trying to sell the vision I had for the company. The beauty is, just like with clients, they start pitching your business back to you. In the end I took in £40k – at a £350k valuation – from four different private investors within my extended network.

 Key note: Saying no is hard

It can be relatively easy for you to get funding from friends and family. The hard part is ensuring the investment won't result in a broken relationship. Therefore, if you think the investment has the potential to destroy your relationship, don't accept money from them! This is the hard part – saying 'no' to people who want to invest because you understand that they don't know what they're doing, or you don't think they can afford to lose the money they want to invest.

The main mistakes when taking money from friends and family

Whilst an investment from friends and family is an attractive source of capital, there are some major mistakes that need to be avoided to reduce the risk of destroying families and friendships.

Top 5 mistakes when taking money from Friends & Family

1. Taking money from someone who doesn't understand how risky startups are
2. Taking money and not explaining the problem of illiquidity
3. Taking money from people who can't afford to lose it
4. You take the money as a loan
5. Too high valuation when taking equity

Mistake 1: Taking money from someone who doesn't understand how risky startups are

The number one mistake, which founders keep making, is taking money from someone who doesn't understand the high level of risk associated with startups. Even when they realise that entrepreneurship is risky, they may believe that because you're their wonderful child or grandchild, you'll be able to beat the odds and become a great success.

Friends and family need to know the reality that most startups fail, and failing means bankruptcy and that not a single euro will make its way back to any of the investors. You have to explain again and again that whilst your business might get big, there is more than a 50 per cent chance the company will go bankrupt, and if it does they won't see a single cent.

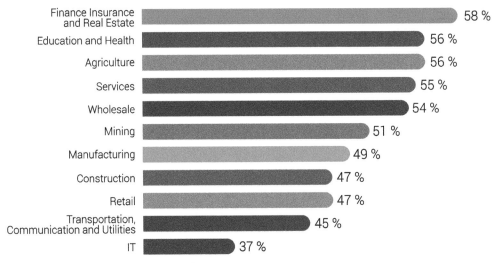

Survival rates for startups after 4 years – per industry

Finance Insurance and Real Estate	58 %
Education and Health	56 %
Agriculture	56 %
Services	55 %
Wholesale	54 %
Mining	51 %
Manufacturing	49 %
Construction	47 %
Retail	47 %
Transportation, Communication and Utilities	45 %
IT	37 %

Source: http://www.statisticbrain.com/startup-failure-by-industry/

If you doubt whether your friends and family really understand the risk, don't take their money. For two reasons:

1. **Ethical** – it's not OK to take money from people who don't really understand the risks

2. **Selfish** – due to broken relationships, your actions will haunt you if/when your startup fails.

Mistake 2: Taking money and not explaining the problem of illiquidity

Even if you have a successful startup, your investors can't get their money out. This often comes as a surprise to friends and family investors who assume you will be an overnight success and will sell the company for €100 million a year down the line. Even if you are successful, that will take five to 10 years. But even in the unlikely event that you build a company worth a hundred million euro, and your investor has three per cent equity and therefore on paper are worth €3 million, it's actually very difficult for them to get that money out. There are two reasons for this:

1. Typically, you sign a shareholder's agreement making it very hard for investors to sell shares because the intention is you invest together and you go out together. So, the investors are in general only allowed to sell shares when all shareholders exit (during a trade-sale or IPO).

2. Even if there is permission to sell to outsiders it will be difficult to find outsiders who want to buy, because the market for unlisted shares is very limited. Your startup may

 © 2017 Nicolaj Højer Nielsen

still be burning a lot of cash. Yes on paper it may be worth €100 million, but the only people actually willing to take that kind of risk are the VCs who are already investing. Your friends and family investors can't expect to easily find another friend or family investor who will pay €3 million to buy out their shares.

VC-backed companies: how many years from when you invest until you exit?

Years from investing to exit (VC-funded companies)

Source: Basil Peters (www.basilpeters.com), based upon data from Jeffries Broadview, Dow Jones Venturesource

If you invest in a company that reaches for the skies and eventually secures venture capital funding, you might be lucky to get a really big exit, but you will also have to be invested in illiquid shares for many years!

The graph below shows an example where a company pursues several rounds of VC financing and the average time it take for founders and early-stage investors from creating or investing in the company until the VC-backed company eventually exits.

Of course it's just an example – your exit could come much faster even if you take VC money – but make sure your investors know what could happen.

Maybe they had a spare €200,000 they wanted to invest in you but they were planning to buy a house with some of that money five years from now. They won't be able to because even if you are successful, the chances of them getting the money out is very low. You will have to explain to them that the money they invest in you will very likely be lost. Alternatively, they won't see any return on their investment for at least 10 years.

Key note: Startup shares are illiquid assets

Make sure your investors are fully aware that the shares in a startup are illiquid. The reality is that when you invest in a startup and it is successful, you need to wait for some kind of exit scenario, an IPO for example, before you can get your money out. Make your investors fully aware of that, and the potential problems this can create for them if they want to take their money out of the investment prematurely.

Mistake 3: Taking money from people who can't afford to lose it

The third mistake founders make is to take money from people who really can't afford to lose it. They may have the money available and they could invest it in you, but if they do and they lose it, will they be able to lead the same lifestyle now and in the future? If they planned on using the money for their retirement fund and they can't travel as much as they'd like if they lose it, then they can't afford it.

My rule of thumb is to only take five per cent net of the investor's equity: if you have a potential investor who is worth a million euros, losing €50,000 is OK because they can continue their lifestyle even if they lose that money. And it's likely there won't be an impact on your friendship.

Mistake 4: You take the money as a loan

The fourth mistake is when the founder accepts funding from friends or family in the form of a loan – say a standard loan with 10 per cent interest. Most private investors who have never operated with startups before think 10 per cent is high interest. Actually, considering the risk in a startup, it's way too low. For most early-stage startups a fair, risk-adjusted interest rate should be more than 50 per cent!

If you don't know if the interest rate you have set is fair, low or high, a quick test is to see if you could borrow the money from the bank at the same rate. If not, then you know you have set the interest rate too low. Of course, a low interest rate is OK if both parties know that, and that the low interest rate reflects that the loan should be seen more as a gift than a loan on commercial terms. The problem arises if they don't know that this is a low interest rate because you aren't giving them an upside.

Let's say your startup becomes the next Google, and the reason you become so successful is that your friend or family member lent you €100,000 that you repaid with interest and said thank you. When they see all the other investors who invested with equity become multi-millionaires and they only get their €100,000 back with interest they might be a little angry.

Mistake 5: Too high valuation when taking equity

The final mistake founders make when raising money from their friends and family is getting too high a valuation. You might be surprised to hear you can get a too-high valuation, but the problem is your friends and family have never done this before. They don't know what is a fair valuation for your type of startup. They don't really understand the risk. So when you go to them with an offer of one per cent of your company for €200,000, they might think that's fine. Which is OK until the next funding round two years later, when the share price has fallen by 50 per cent even if you're very successful. Your friends and family investors might think you've cheated them. You can try to fix that by giving them more shares, but you still have the problem that they think they didn't get a fair valuation.

This is fine if they know it might happen, if they're looking to help you and accept that the money they provide is more of a gift than an investment. If not, you should try to overcome the problem with a convertible loan; a popular solution in the US but less so in Europe.

Convertible loans. A convertible loan is essentially a normal loan from a lender to your company, with typical interest of five to 10 per cent, but it also comes with an upside to the lender who can convert the loan into equity later on.

Convertible loans provide friends and family investors the right to convert the loan to equity at a discount compared to the share price set in later rounds.

Most often the two parties are too closely related to be able to actually negotiate terms (it's really hard to negotiate with one of your best friends). What you can do is agree that it's a loan and if the startup needs more funding, the lender will get a discount compared to later investors.

That way you may start by accepting a normal loan for €100,000. Later on, when a VC fund wants to invest €2 million at a per share of €100, that gives the lender the right to convert the loan into shares with a discount compared to the new funding round. That way you will avoid the problems associated with two amateurs negotiating a price for the shares based on not enough experience and too little information. The discount will typically end up in the 15 to 25 per cent range compared to the share price the new investor pays.

Take-away points

For most startups, friends and family are an important source of funding. If they trust you they are most willing to invest in you very early on. But there are many pitfalls and if not enough attention was paid to potential problems, broken relationships are the result.

Most non-professional investors don't really know if your business has a good chance of success or not, and they are blinded by your personal relationship. Think really hard before accepting funding from friends and family. Make sure they know the high risk and that they will have to wait 10 years or so for any return on their investment to be paid out.

 © 2017 Nicolaj Højer Nielsen

© 2017 Nicolaj Højer Nielsen

─────── Chapter 7: ───────
Startup Accelerators

A startup accelerator might be the tool you need to advance your startup to the point you're able to attract other kinds of funding. In this chapter you will learn about the benefits and downsides of being accepted into an accelerator programme and what you should be aware of before applying.

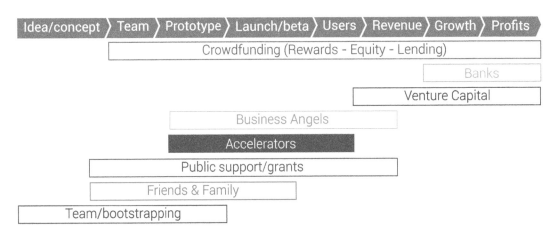

What is a startup accelerator?

Accelerator programmes are essentially *startup factories*. They speed up the process of creating successful startups.

An accelerator is typically a three- to six-month programme involving intensive, on-site training and mentoring of the startups. As a startup, you are accepted into a cohort – much like being accepted into a business school – where you work with all the other startups that have been accepted, attend workshops on how to build your business, and receive mentoring from experienced entrepreneurs. You are working towards what is often called a *demo day* when a lot of influential people, VCs, investors and business angels will be present and each startup will showcase their project and how far along they are in the process.

Accelerators vs. incubators

You may wonder what the difference is between an accelerator and incubator and for good reason because the differences aren't clear cut. Whilst accelerators are relatively new, incubators have been around for a while. Normally, you don't go to an incubator for just three to six months – it's essentially your workplace. Incubators build services on top of their office spaces to add value for the startups, which can include mentoring and workshops. But an incubator is typically less intensive, longer term and more focused on creating a good office environment than an accelerator. It helps you connect with other startups, but is still just an office with added benefits.

 © 2017 Nicolaj Højer Nielsen

	INCUBATOR	ACCELERATOR
Offering	Office space and shared admin. Mentoring in varying degrees	Teaching, networking, mentoring, help getting investors
Commitment from startups to join	Normally no specific requirements regarding work load	Most accelerators only accept startups where founders work full-time
Co-working space included	Yes	Yes
Term	No fixed term. Rent space often for a longer period of time	Startups accepted in 1-2 cohorts per year. Programme typically runs for 3-6 months
Payment	No equity. Rent office-space (sometimes offered for free)	Equity (3-8%), getting €10,000-50,000 in return

Startup accelerators are a relatively new type of company (pioneered by Y Combinator in 2005 and TechStars in 2006) from the US. They have now spread all over the world and thousands of different startup accelerators are accepting startups in their cohorts.

The table below contains a selection of the most renowned accelerator programmes with active programmes in the EU. Many more accelerators are being created each month, and many of the famous US accelerators might have created EU programmes by the time you read this!

NAME	WEBSITE
Tech Stars	http://www.techstars.com/
Startupbootcamp	https://www.startupbootcamp.org/
Seed Camp	http://seedcamp.com/
500 Startups	http://500.co/
Mass Challenge	http://masschallenge.org/
Accelerace	https://www.accelerace.dk/

What's the business model of an accelerator?

How do accelerators make money? Some are financed partly or fully by public money, but the majority are private organisations. Privately-run accelerators provide you with a bit of cash — typically between €10,000 to €25,000 — mentoring and training, workshops and a small office.

And for that you pay three to eight per cent of your equity.

This is the real reason accelerators exist. Unlike some incubators, they don't want to make money on training or office space. They hope that among their students are the next DropBox or Airbnb, two of the most famous examples of companies that have participated in accelerator programmes and become big. The accelerators bank on owning five per cent of the next Dropbox.

 Key note: Accelerators behaving like small VCs

The basic model of accelerators emerged because they thought they could make money by having five per cent of a hundred startups if a few became very successful. What the accelerators realised – like many business angels have – is that they also need their own funds, otherwise they quickly get diluted in the success stories. For example, they might have five per cent of the next Dropbox, but then along comes a big VC, and because the accelerator doesn't have money to invest, they suddenly find themselves owning one and not five per cent. Many accelerators are building up more funds so they can co-invest with VCs that come in later. Because of this, the distinction between accelerators and VC funds is becoming blurred.

Why include accelerators in a book about funding?

You might wonder why we're discussing accelerators when the funding provided by them is so small. Such small amounts can often be raised from friends and family or business angels, and in most cases the cost will be less than what accelerators demand.

But the real value that accelerators can bring is not the initial funding they provide, but that the accelerators are the gateway to further financing after demo day.

Take as an example the statistics below from Startupbootcamp, one of the leading EU-based startup accelerators. Of the 345 companies that have participated in their accelerator programmes across the EU, 229 (73%) raised follow-on funding. The average funding raised per startup was €734,000.

Are these statistics biased in the sense the best accelerators can pick and choose among multiple startups so they therefore get the best ones – those that would have raised capital even if they didn't participate in the programme? Yes, most likely, but despite this bias there's the feeling that participating in accelerator programmes can have a large, positive impact on the startup's ability to raise follow-on funding.

 © 2017 Nicolaj Højer Nielsen

Statistics from Startupbootcamp

	NUMBER	PERCENTAGE
Total Startups	345	
In Program	32	9%
Graduated:	313	
– Active	247	79%
– Acquired	10	3%
– Folded	56	18%
Graduated Funded	229	73%
Avg. Raised per Startup	€734K	

Source: https://www.startupbootcamp.org/

When and what do accelerators invest in?

Typically, accelerators are interested in early-stage startups, roughly at the same stage as an early-stage business angel would invest. Since accelerators only give startups a small amount of money, they know they can't target startups that already are far into their development because they will never give five per cent of their company in return for €20,000.

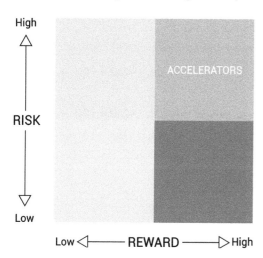

At the same time, accelerators aren't interested in just one person with an idea. As with early-stage business angels, to get accepted into an accelerator programme you need to have assembled a great team, have a good understanding of the market, have a problem to be solved (which you can show you know how to solve), and be able to provide evidence of the market. If you have a few users or customers already, that's a big plus.

Accelerators go for high risk/high reward startups. They are willing to take the same high risks as a VC fund, but unlike VCs – who are looking for a more mature company with a proven business model – accelerators go in much earlier because of the small-scale investment required.

They are on the lookout for candidates that can become big, very fast, because they own only about five per cent of that company. That's why most accelerators are looking for technology-based startups, especially within software, and to a lesser extent also hardware and health.

The graph below illustrates the portfolio of Seedcamp in terms of its different industry sectors, and also how the top industry sector has changed over time.

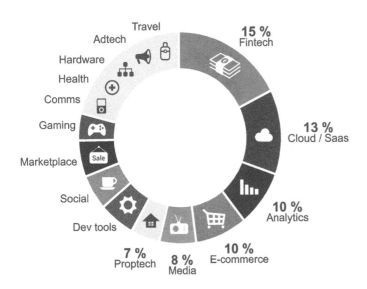

What's in the Seedcamp Portfolio

Source: Seedcamp

Top industry / Year

2015	Fintech
2014	Media
2013	Marketplace
2012	Fintech
2011	Cloud
2010	Cloud
2009	Adtech
2008	Analytics
2007	Analytics

 © 2017 Nicolaj Højer Nielsen

Key note: Don't join an accelerator to get the money

You should not consider joining an accelerator just to get your hands on €20,000. This money is basically provided to ensure you and your team have enough to survive on for the length of the programme. And the money will burn very fast because the accelerators expect you to relocate the team to the place where the programme takes place.

What's the value to the startup?

Here are the three reasons you should consider an accelerator programme:

Benefits of startup accelerators

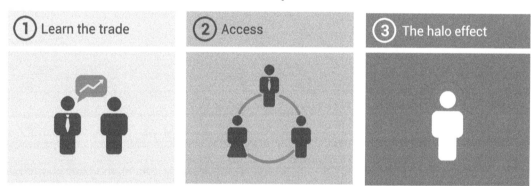

1. Learn the trade

One of the key benefits of being part of an accelerator programme is the opportunity to learn hands-on entrepreneurship from experienced mentors and peers. The value proposition of the accelerator is that whilst they maybe only have three or four full-time people employed, they have 50-plus senior mentors, some of whom are investors or serial entrepreneurs. These mentors host workshops and give free advice on how to build your company.

You can see the accelerator programme as an intensive training camp where you are doing the equivalent of a hands-on MBA in entrepreneurship with like-minded people. This is very valuable to first-time entrepreneurs but if you have already run four startups, you need to ask yourself if participating in an accelerator programme is worth it. Most likely it won't be. You have probably made all the mistakes necessary to have already learned what the mentors will teach you.

2. Access

If you're a first-time entrepreneur, you probably don't have access to 50 serial entrepreneurs or VCs you can talk to whenever you want. Connecting with successful entrepreneurs and VCs is one of the key benefits of an accelerator programme.

You become part of a community during the programme which provides the kind and level of access that would be difficult to achieve anywhere else. That's not to say you couldn't achieve this on your own, but we all know how busy investors and experienced entrepreneurs are. It's a lot easier when the accelerator has already invited them to spend an evening with you.

One of the key events during the accelerator programme is the 'investor night', where the accelerator makes sure hundreds of business angels and venture capital partners attend your presentation. Such attention is almost impossible to get for the average first-time entrepreneur, and is a major reason behind the very positive data on investments in companies that have participated in accelerator programmes.

3. The halo effect

The third value is in the kudos your startup might get by being part of an accelerator. This is only valid for the top accelerators worldwide and it's like a self-fulfilling prophecy. If you've been accepted into a great accelerator, you must be good so VCs and business angels will want to talk to you and give you their money.

You can see this 'brand' you get from the top accelerators as the startup version of getting an MBA from a top-tier business school like INSEAD. Do you become smarter/better through the teaching they provide? Most likely. But even if you don't, people will probably think you're smarter since you were accepted into INSEAD and therefore you have a higher chance of success.

There is little doubt that if you are a first-time entrepreneur and get accepted into one of the top accelerators, it will create value for you. Not only in terms of know-how or access, but the brand value alone of having graduated from Tech Stars or Y Combinator (for example) makes up for your time and the equity!

Case study: Why 3DHubs joined an accelerator

The 3DHubs platform connects people who want to make 3D prints with local 3D printer owners. Since its launch, 3DHubs has experienced a huge growth in users and connected print hubs (over ten thousand production locations in more than 140 countries), making them the world's largest network of 3D printers.

 © 2017 Nicolaj Højer Nielsen

The initial idea for 3DHubs came to life in a conversation between two co-workers then working at 3D Systems; Bram de Zwart and Brain Garret. They realised there was an absence of infrastructure supporting the future promise of 3D printing. Bram and Brian quit their jobs early in 2013 and launched 3DHubs in the Netherlands and Belgium a few months later.

When 3DHubs launched, users joined the platform within the first week. Only a few months later it had grown to become the largest 3D printing platform in Europe. By this time, the startup had joined the Rockstart Accelerator and the huge traction quickly got the attention of investors who were connected to the accelerator programme.

Bram de Zwart explains: We got in touch with a lot of investors at the Rockstart Accelerator. The accelerator gets 400 applications and only admits 10 startups into the programme. This attracts a lot of investors since they save a lot of time and don't have to filter out the not so ambitious or untalented people.

The huge investor interest soon turned into an initial seed round and was backed by two Dutch business angels and two micro VC funds. What happened was that we had already agreed on an investment with the Dutch investors when Balderton [VC] contacted us at the last moment and said they wanted to participate. Actually, it was so last minute I had to ask the Dutch investors if they were willing to decrease their size of investment so we could make some space for Balderton.

I think one of the best decisions we made was to apply for Rockstart Accelerator. Joining an accelerator can not only help to propel the development of your startup but also give you valuable access and exposure to potential investors.

Downsides of being in an accelerator programme

Now that we've looked at what an accelerator programme can bring you, who they're looking for, and when they invest, let's look at the possible downsides.

Downsides of startup accelerators

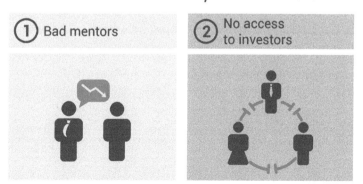

1. Bad mentors

The first problem with an accelerator programme is bad mentors. Mentorship is the cornerstone of basically all accelerator programmes. The reason why only a handful of full-time accelerator employees can handle 10 to 15 startups per semester is down to the mentors associated with the accelerator.

Advice from a former partner at an accelerator: Do your due diligence!

Lars Buch, former head of Startupbootcamp Mobile accelerator, explains:

One of the biggest mistakes startups make when applying to startup accelerators is not doing their own due diligence on the accelerator! The startups should validate the performance of the specific accelerator before spending time applying to it. The best accelerators openly share their performance data – survival rates of startups, how much investment the startups attract, employee growth rates, etc.

If the accelerator doesn't share this data the startup should think twice. If they're still interested, they should confront the accelerator and ask for the information directly. There are 2000 accelerators out there, and many don't provide the value startups hope for. By performing due diligence, startups can minimise the risk of wasting time, money and equity on an accelerator that doesn't work!

The problem is all accelerators basically chase the same small pool of mentors (ideally serial entrepreneurs and investors) with the right experience, track record and credibility for providing mentorship. But these people are often very busy and reluctant to spend their evenings with you since they have a huge deal flow already.

This point leads to another downside, which is the risk that the mentorship you will get from the average accelerator (not the top tier accelerators) is mainly from corporate people or advisors (consultants or accountants, for example) who see this as a way to get into the startup community and maybe invest time/money in a startup. They could well be honest people with good motives, but they could also be people who are bored at work or consultants who want to create a new deal flow, with little experience to share.

 © 2017 Nicolaj Højer Nielsen

Key note: Check out their mentors!

Check out the mentors of the accelerator you are considering applying to. Who are they? Have they created startups themselves? If possible, talk to startups that have already participated in the specific accelerator – what kind of mentorship did they receive? This isn't necessary if you're accepted into one of the top-tier accelerators where the mentors are very experienced. But it's essential if you're considering joining one of the hundreds of other accelerators out there.

2. No access to investors

The second potential downside is that you don't get access to the investors you were promised. With the exponential increase in the number of accelerator programmes, many don't have that access because the same 20 VCs or the same hundred business angels simply don't have time to connect and engage with each one.

If you participate in an accelerator programme that isn't top tier, you may not get access to the investors you hoped for because business angels and venture capitalists won't prioritise their participation in that particular accelerator's investor night. The fact you graduated from an average accelerator won't help you much either when you try to book meetings with investors. They simply won't believe your startup is any more interesting than the average one.

 Key note: Do they provide access to investors?

Check out the specific accelerator's ability to connect startups with investors. Ask for the investor statistics from past batches – how many of the startups raised follow-on funding? From whom did they raise it and how much? If the accelerator says they don't have the data or aren't willing to share it, this is a warning sign, perhaps even a red flag. A key part of the accelerator's value proposition is the ability to help startups attract follow-on funding!

How do you get on an accelerator programme?

If you've decided that an accelerator programme is the right move for your startup, then how do you get accepted into an accelerator programme and which programme should you apply to?

1. What's right for you

Location – The network and access you'll get will depend on your specific location. If you apply to an accelerator in Amsterdam, for example, there's a big chance the majority of the network and mentoring will be in the Netherlands, although there will also be people flying in from Western Europe.

You also need to think long-term. Why build a network in a city which you plan to move from afterwards? If you want to build your company in London it might not make sense to be in an Amsterdam-based accelerator because then you have to convince investors (who may be from Amsterdam) to invest in a London-based startup. It might be better to apply to accelerators where you will most likely build your startup afterwards.

Broad versus specialised accelerators – Is there a cluster for your industry that makes sense for you? Part of the trend with accelerators has been to become more specialised by providing accelerator programmes within specific niche industries. There could be accelerators for finance and technology companies, for medical companies, or for hardware companies. You should consider if it makes sense for you to apply to one of those because there is then a greater chance you will receive specialised advice you can use. If you're working with financial technology, it might make sense for you to place yourself in London, home to one of the biggest financial clusters in the world.

2. Application process

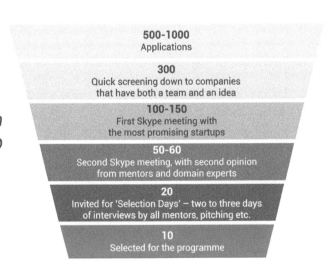

Typical application process for startup accelerator

© 2017 Nicolaj Højer Nielsen

All accelerators follow a formal application process where you fill in an online form with your details including your education and information about your team. Accelerators might ask for extra information (perhaps a video application), but the process is similar for most of them.

Of course, they can't meet and greet all 500 initial applicants. They want to quickly get from 500 to 100 candidates without interviewing them, and this is what the written application is for. Competition for places is fierce and you need to be prepared to allocate time and effort into making your application excellent. In my experience, accelerators only spend minutes per application deciding if it will be a 'yes' or 'no'.

The remaining hundred or so candidates will be subject to a more in-depth screening – perhaps a Skype interview to get a better sense of the people behind the startup. After that the field of candidates might have been reduced to 20 or 30. These will be invited to an in-person interview or to selection camps where the evaluators will spend a few hours or even a day with each team. Based on the results of the camp, the accelerator will choose the 10 or so candidates who will be invited into the programme.

3. How to come through the pre-screening process

I have interviewed a lot of the decision makers on these accelerator programmes and asked them what common mistakes they see startups make during the selection process. Here is what I learnt:

1. Maturity. The startup isn't mature enough. Because so many startups apply, those with only an idea to present will be discarded. Accelerators want to see projects and teams that can show evidence of what they can do and that they can do it. One person and an idea isn't enough; you'll get rejected right away. The simple fact you are one person gives a clear negative signal there must be something wrong; you are too early for the accelerator programme because you haven't got a team together, or something is wrong with your idea because nobody wants to join your team.

The accelerators (especially the top ones) can afford to be very picky and will want to see some validation of the maturity of the project, either on the market or the team side. On the market side, you might have a prototype or some users, on the team side you might have three or four cool people who have left great jobs to join you. Lesson here is: if you're too early or don't have a team, don't apply.

2. No pain. The accelerators feel you have an invented problem. There is no pain for the customers, so the problem you believe a lot of customers are having doesn't exist. When I asked accelerators how they decided whether they believed the problem existed, they frequently said it was both a gut feeling and also what they had seen in the past. Many of them are experienced and have already seen other applicants who've tried to solve a similar problem, and they've seen that the problem wasn't big enough.

It could also be that the niche is simply too small. Remember, they're looking for something that can attract VC funding and it has to be something they believe can be big one year from now.

3. Lack of market understanding. Accelerators receive and read hundreds of applications. If they have been operating for more than just a few years they might have seen many thousand startups applying to their programme. They know what's going on in the market; they know many of the startups in the US and Europe. They may hear a startup claim they're the first in the world to do something, but have seen three other startups already doing it. When startups claim something like this, it shows accelerators the people behind the startup have not done their homework. It's OK that there are other startups trying to solve the same problem, as long as you show how you're different.

4. Way too far. Some of the startups that apply are too far down the road to be of interest for an accelerator programme. If you've already taken part in an accelerator programme, or have already raised €500,000, you shouldn't be willing to give up eight per cent of your equity for €20,000. If you are, either there is something wrong and you know it, or there's something wrong and you don't yet know it. Either way it's a problem and you won't be selected.

5. You're not serious. This is about the sum of many small signs. If you're asked to make a video in the application process about your team and product and you don't make it, or no one in your team is working full-time at your startup, these are small signs that make the accelerator worried you are not serious. They want you to jump in now and show you're working day and night on your startup. Of course, you might need to have a part-time job as a bartender to pay the bills, but you need to show you really want this. If you don't put in the time necessary for making a killer application and a professional looking video to go with it, why should the accelerator believe you have what it takes to build a successful business?

6. The financial part. What accelerators are really afraid of is that you will run out of money halfway through the process. They know they are only providing you with €20,000 and so they need to see you have a run rate that is long enough. Accelerators know you won't be able to secure follow-on funding the day after the end-of-programme. They need to know you have enough money to last until an investor comes in, and they know this is not possible if your team is too big and/or has a too-high monthly burn rate.

 © 2017 Nicolaj Højer Nielsen

Advice from an accelerator: Be committed!

Cristobal Alonso is CEO of the startup accelerator Startup Wise Guys and has shared here what he believes is the biggest mistake startups make when applying to accelerators:

You shouldn't waste your time applying to a startup accelerator if you are not committed!

Many founders are applying to accelerators just to try their luck and are not fully committed to their startup. Some might have a good idea and background, but they're not ready to quit their day job and fully commit to their startup.

The whole idea with a startup accelerator is that you are fully dedicated to the startup and work full-time in the months where you are accepted into the accelerator. So don't waste your own time – and the time of the accelerators reviewing your application – if you don't really want to do it full-time! We *will* find out during the selection process!

4. How to get to the final 10

Startups that pass with flying colours on each of the above six points will be well on their way to become one of the hundred or so candidates who get through to the next round – and who may eventually become one of the selected 10 candidates.

Two factors stand out when it comes to making it all the way.

The team. Accelerators know it's all about the people and will ask themselves if your team has what it takes to be successful. They will use a mixture of tests and interviews to evaluate your team's skills and aptitudes. Do you have the formal skills? Do they trust you have what it takes? Do you indicate you can actively work together as a team? Are you willing to think long term on building agreements so you can kick out founders who don't perform? Are you fun to work with? You might be cool, you might have a great product, but if you appear difficult to get along with and collaborate with, you won't get through. The accelerator will also become your shareholder and knows if your personality is against you, it will be hard for you to get follow-on funding because it's all about people.

The unfair advantage. The second thing accelerators are looking for is what VCs call the 'unfair advantage', a unique feature of your business that isn't easily duplicated. There might be a customer problem that you're able to solve, but do you really have what it takes to resolve

© 2017 Nicolaj Højer Nielsen   99

it? Are there clear indications that your approach, technology or software constitute a unique solution? Do potential investors really trust you have what it takes to be a global winner?

Take-away points

Don't go to an accelerator for the small amounts of money they are investing themselves. The main role of accelerators, in a funding perspective, it to be a stepping-stone towards further financing from business angels and VCs.

Accelerators are looking for much the same in startups as VCs, but accelerators go in much earlier. However, don't make the common mistake of applying to an accelerator when you only have an idea. Go when you have a team and some kind of indication you have a solution for the customer problem you've identified.

But before you do, evaluate the pros and cons – is the level of mentoring, training and access to investors enough value for you to give away your time and equity to an accelerator?

If it's of value to you, only apply to an accelerator programme if you have the time and interest to do it properly. Otherwise, you will only be accepted into third tier accelerators who might not be able to create the value you're looking for.

 © 2017 Nicolaj Højer Nielsen

© 2017 Nicolaj Højer Nielsen

Chapter 8:
Business Angels

Who will invest in your company after you've bootstrapped? Many founders conclude that business angels (private investors who invest their own money in startups) are next. This is how business angels differ from VC funds that manage and invest other people's money. In this chapter we will investigate the best ways to catch a business angel and how to avoid the most common mistakes entrepreneurs make when looking for business angel investments in their company.

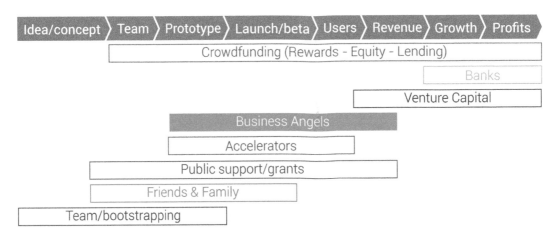

When do business angels invest?

Business angels are typically the first investors in startups and invest much earlier than venture capitalists. Unlike with venture capitalists, you don't need massive existing revenue or millions of users for getting a business angel interested in your company. However, most business angels don't invest when you only have a business idea in your head or down on paper in a business plan. They want you to have taken the first steps.

This is especially true for projects with a high degree of technology risk and still in the research and development phase. In many cases, the business angel doesn't have expert knowledge about your technology and will have a hard time evaluating risks. Therefore, many angels prefer not to invest when you are too far away from the market (typically more than a few months before launch) and haven't demonstrated your technology actually works.

Case study: Franco Gianera - entrepreneur turned business angel

amazonbuyvip

A former business consultant for Andersen, Franco Gianera left a CIO position at Adecco to follow his entrepreneurial dreams by

 © 2017 Nicolaj Højer Nielsen

co-founding Buy Vip (the Spanish premium clothing retailer bought by Amazon for €70 million in 2010). Today Franco works as an angel investor with investment into a variety of startups (for example, Smarto, Spotlime and Marchetti Atelier). He explains:

Throughout the course of my career, I have acquired a quite varied mix of competencies. Business consulting strengthened my managerial skills and while with Adecco I gained an international perspective and network. I now want to make the most of this wealth of experience, participating in the lives of tech startups that operate in sectors I know.

At this moment, I'm investing on a 'spot' basis: I select companies I like, with teams I like, operating in industries where I have some expertise. I also provide mentoring and advice. In the future my goal is to invest in a more structured way, but for now I invest on an ad-hoc basis when I meet interesting startups.

Why do business angels invest?

The reason business angels are willing to take higher risks than other types of investors by investing earlier in the process can be explained by looking into the reasons they get involved in startups. This understanding will help you pitch your business proposal in the right way.

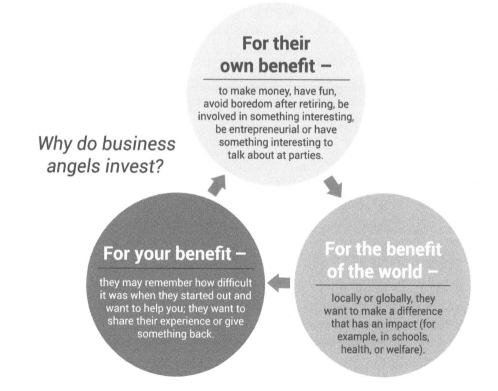

Why do business angels invest?

For their own benefit –
to make money, have fun, avoid boredom after retiring, be involved in something interesting, be entrepreneurial or have something interesting to talk about at parties.

For the benefit of the world –
locally or globally, they want to make a difference that has an impact (for example, in schools, health, or welfare).

For your benefit –
they may remember how difficult it was when they started out and want to help you; they want to share their experience or give something back.

Here's an example. In one company I invested in, one of the business angels is worth €200 million. Why would a business person with a net worth of €200 million invest in a startup which only has the potential to earn them an additional €5 or €10 million? For most people (myself included) a €5 – 10 million profit would be a great reason to invest. But if you're already worth €200 million, you would easily make €10 million per year if you invest your equity passively in the stock market or other asset classes. So why invest in risky startups? Because the financial gains are not the real motivation for his investments in startups.

There are three main reasons for business angels to invest in startups and getting rich is rarely the main motivation.

Business angel: Why do I invest in startups?

Tommy Andersen is a tech entrepreneur and business angel who has invested in early-stage startups within multiple industries. He explains:

So why do I invest in startups as a business angel? Well, primarily because I want to give back to the startup community and pay it forward. Of course, I also want to make a good deal and hope the company I invest in will become immensely successful and provide a solid return on my investment, but I know of the risk of investing in early-stage companies, and that I would most likely get a better return on investment if I invested in other assets. Angel-investing isn't for the faint of heart and I recognise that.

Finding business angels for Recon Instruments

When I helped Recon Instruments secure seed funding, I reached out to several potential business angels in my network. During that process, I targeted angels who had previously invested in tech startups and thus knew the risk of investing in an early-stage technology company like Recon Instruments.

This way, I could focus on those who were most willing to take risks, and not waste my time on angels who either don't invest in technology companies or only invest later when the company has a less risky profile. I also tried to target angels who had a personal interest in skiing. I assumed they would easily grasp the value proposition of Recon Instruments (ski-goggles with built-in heads-up display).

106 © 2017 Nicolaj Højer Nielsen

Til: 'Nicolaj Højer Nielsen'
Emne: RE: INSEAD - Recon Instruments (skiing + angel investment)

Dear Nicolaj

Looks fun and I hope potentially profitable. Please send me the exec summary.

Regards
Michael

The response above from one such business angel sums up the thinking of many business angels when they evaluate investment opportunities: it has to be fun – and 'potentially profitable'. The message is this: you rarely convince a business angel to invest if you're only offering profit to them.

 Key note: Business angels don't only care about money!

You need to understand why angels invest before you can get them to invest in you.

Most entrepreneurs, when seeking funding, make the mistake of thinking that business angels invest mainly to make money. Of course, that's one of their reasons but many business angels are rich already or know they could increase their wealth by investing on the stock market or in other asset classes (for example, land or property). You will increase your chance of a successful pitch to business angels if you understand why they're interested in startups – and it's rarely only for financial gain!

What do business angels invest in?

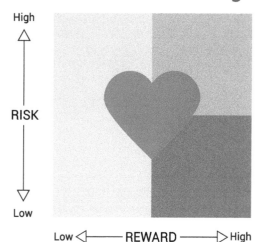

So which type of investment cases are business angels looking for? Are they looking for the very high risk and high reward cases that can bring in hundreds of millions of euros just like VC funds?

No. Business angels invest all over the place, both in 'the next Google' and also in businesses perceived to be low risk/low reward. Some business angels even invest in cases where they believe the actual risk is far higher than the potential reward justifies (high risk/low reward), but they still want to invest for other reasons than the financial outcome.

Different types of business angels

One reason why business angels invest so differently is that they are not a homogenous group but a very diverse mix of people with only their interest in investing in startups in common. Business angels are not just serial-entrepreneurs who have become multi-millionaires!

It's important for entrepreneurs looking for financing to understand the differences between the different groups of business angels, which is the reason they make investment decisions so differently from each other.

In simple terms, there are three types of business angels:

	NEW ANGELS	BA NETWORKS	SUPER ANGELS
Role	Typically passive but often wants to be involved on an ad-hoc basis; you have the chance to get valuable know-how	Varies but one angel often acts as lead and is typically very active while other investors are more passive	Typically actively uses their own network and personal brand to help make the startup a success
Alone or in consortia	Usually invests alone but you can pool them together to reach your funding goal, e.g. use 3-5 different investors	Most prefer to make consortia with other angels from same network: spread risk, more power	Invest alone or with other investors they trust (both private and institutional investors)
Investment size	Typically, less than €50,000 per person per round	Varies, but a typical investment round comprises of €100,000-500,000 invested by 2-5 angels together	Varies, up to €1 million per company, but more often €100,000-250,000 per investment round
Industry focus	None, but much harder to convince investors if the technology is so specialised they don't understand the problem or solution	Varies, but normally at least one person in the consortia has the industry know-how necessary to convince them	Experienced entrepreneurs who typically invest in the same industries as those in which they made their own money
How to find them	Your extended network, i.e. friends of friends; typically don't consider themselves business angels but have equity from successful corporate careers or startups	BA network web pages; you can upload a deck and ask to pitch in front of the angels; better chance of success if you are introduced to one of the angels beforehand	Articles and public information on people who have built successful companies, and invested in startups; better to be introduced via mutual contacts

 © 2017 Nicolaj Højer Nielsen

Business angel networks

Some business angels prefer to invest in collaboration with other angels. This is called 'syndication' and is often done via business angel networks all over the world, where a group of angels meets informally on a regular basis to discuss potential investment opportunities.

So why do business angels prefer to invest together instead of alone?

Why do business angels prefer to invest together?

1. **It works as a deal aggregator.** By being part of a network the angel gets access to startups seeking capital outside their personal network and gets a number of investment opportunities with limited effort.

2. **The angel has limited funds.** One of the key differences between business angels and other types of investors is that the amount of money most angels have to invest is limited. Being part of a business angel network (and investing with other members) enables the angel to spread their investments over several different startups and mitigate some of the risks.

3. **More eyes on the same deal.** Angels (unlike venture capitalist funds) don't have a large team of people to help analyse the deal; they are most often alone. But by engaging in the business angel network they can discuss the potential deal with other members and co-invest with them, thereby limiting the perceived risk of investing in the company.

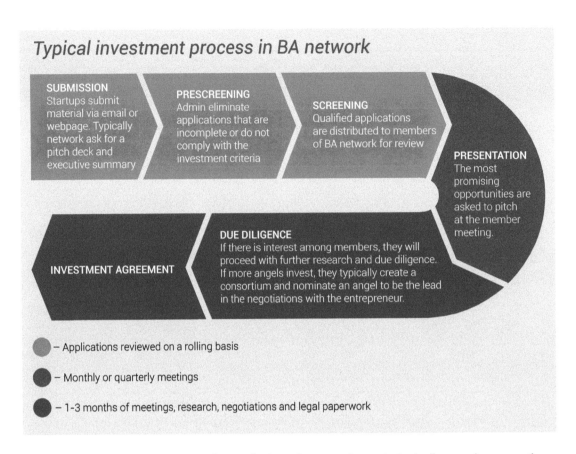

Typical investment process in BA network

SUBMISSION
Startups submit material via email or webpage. Typically network ask for a pitch deck and executive summary

PRESCREENING
Admin eliminate applications that are incomplete or do not comply with the investment criteria

SCREENING
Qualified applications are distributed to members of BA network for review

PRESENTATION
The most promising opportunities are asked to pitch at the member meeting.

DUE DILIGENCE
If there is interest among members, they will proceed with further research and due diligence. If more angels invest, they typically create a consortium and nominate an angel to be the lead in the negotiations with the entrepreneur.

INVESTMENT AGREEMENT

- Applications reviewed on a rolling basis

- Monthly or quarterly meetings

- 1-3 months of meetings, research, negotiations and legal paperwork

Business angel networks are made up of a broad range of people including senior executives, lawyers, accountants, bankers, entrepreneurs, and people with 'old money'. What they have in common is entrepreneurship and desire to invest some of their equity into startups.

They're likely to be looking for a good financial return of typically at least three to five times the money they invested if they're looking at an early-stage company. However for the majority of members they are honestly interested in s and the financial return is only a minor part of the reason they invest and are members.

Most of them are also experienced in business angel investments. They have done several deals (alone or in a network) and even if they haven't, they quickly learn the dos and don'ts from other network members. That's why entrepreneurs approaching members of these networks will quickly realise that negotiations with regards to investment terms and valuation can be relatively tough. These business angels bring a lot of experience to the table and know from other deals what a 'fair price' is.

To locate your local business angel network simply do a Google search in your local language for something like 'business angel network' AND the name of your country or city (if you live in a larger city). Alternatively, go to the website of the European Business Angel Association

 © 2017 Nicolaj Højer Nielsen

(www.eban.org) and search for members in your home country.

Case study: How Spotlime got funded via an Italian business angel network

Francesco Rieppi explains how he used funding from a BA network to grow Spotlime, a mobile ticketing app for last-minute events in Milan, Italy:

In 2013 I worked in Berlin and I used to go back to Milan only once or twice a month. Having worked in Berlin on the case of an e-ticketing platform, I saw a huge, untapped potential in the Italian events sector due to its high unsold shares. After building a minimum viable product that scored a good conversion rate, I quit my job and flew back to Milan where I started to contact clubs and events managers and signed the first deals. In early 2014 the beta version of Spotlime was published on the app stores with a daily selection of the coolest events in Milan.

In 2014 we won a competition and joined the Mind The Bridge Startup School in San Francisco for three weeks. We never joined an accelerator programme in Italy and we didn't really need it. We were four co-founders with diverse backgrounds and complementary skills, ranging from marketing to design and computer engineering, so we covered all the skills needed to build and manage the platform.

Instead, we got a seed investment of €200.000 from IBAN (an association of Italian business angels) and one of the co-founders of Fastweb. At Spotlime we had cross-boundary skills and lots of experience in the ticketing business, which was crucial in getting funded by the angel investors. I think a good pitch matters more than any business plan at this early stage. You have to transmit your vision very clearly and 'sell' it to the investor, showing traction and the strength of the team.

Super angels

Not all angels prefer to invest via formal business angel networks. This is especially true for the so-called 'super angels'. These are high net worth individuals who have typically earned their money via their own ventures (exits) and decided to invest a significant portion of their proceeds in new startups.

Some have investment as their main job (operating like a micro-VC fund), while others maintain jobs (often as CEOs of new startups) while operating as business angels on the side.

Super angels are different from typical angel network members in that:

1. They believe (often rightfully so) they have a huge deal flow directly via their own network so they have no need to source deals via business angel networks.

2. They often have relatively high net worth and are willing to fund the entire investment round themselves in early-stage startups. They don't see a need to syndicate via networks (if they want to syndicate, they often have huge professional networks they can co-invest with).

3. They often invest in the same industries in which they have made their own money. They know who to call to check the validity of a business idea or team. Many feel they don't need to get more eyes on the deal from the members of a business angel network. They are confident investors and can do the deals themselves.

Case study: SimpleSite got a €2 million investment from a super angel

Business angel investments are often viewed as small and used to start the business almost from scratch. But you can also find business angels with much deeper pockets who invest later in the process. SimpleSite bootstrapped at first, and then after proving their business model, got a huge investment from a local super angel.

Morten Elk started SimpleSite in 2003 with the goal of offering easy web-building tools for micro-businesses. Its business model is the software as a service (SaaS) model, in which they advertise online and get clicks from interested users. Some of these create a free website and some eventually become paying subscribers. SimpleSite grew organically until 2012 when it had annual revenue of €4.5 million, 29 employees and a net early-stage of approximately zero (it invested all potential profits into future growth via online marketing).

Morten Elk explains their rationale for taking in a business angel as investor:

The key thing to understand about our business model is that we effectively 'buy' customers with a given lifetime value through marketing. To have profitable growth, we must, on average, pay less for the customers than the lifetime revenue they give us

 © 2017 Nicolaj Højer Nielsen

(minus variable costs, naturally). In 2012, it was clear we knew a few things very well:

1. We knew how to calculate the lifetime value (LTV) and acquisition costs per customer (CAC).

2. We were making very good business in a few markets and we had proved that by translating to more languages we could address more markets with exactly the same 'money machine'. So that was a tremendous growth opportunity.

3. We knew that to fully exploit that opportunity, we would need extra short-term funding to translate to more languages (a fixed investment) and start marketing in those markets.

We got in touch with a local investor, Kaare Danielsen, founder of Jobindex – the job advertising platform Kaare built from scratch that got listed on the Copenhagen Stock Exchange. I lived in the same student hall as Kaare when I was studying, but we'd never been closer than that. But we knew each other because we were both entrepreneurs living in Copenhagen and sometimes attended the same events. I was therefore comfortable reaching out to Kaare and started by pitching to him via email.

Kaare invested €2 million in SimpleSite; money that enabled us to get off the ground with international scaling much faster than if it had been self-funded, and enabled us to grow the business from €4.5 million in revenue in 2012 to close to €10 million in 2016.

I believe Kaare only dared to invest such a large amount because we knew our business model and metrics extremely well, and the funding was clearly to be used for a non-speculative scaling of a model with known metrics, performance and profitability.

From the investor point of view, that obviously lowers risk and makes it easier for the startup to close funding on comfortable terms. So although not all funding-seeking businesses can obtain the kind of clarity about metrics and business model we had, it really helps if you can.

New Angels

One of the biggest mistakes founders make when looking for business angel financing is to only focus their attention on angels who invest via business angel networks, and the super angels they know from the media (and TV shows like *Dragon's Den*). What they miss is an important group of business angels – the group I call 'new angels'.

New angels are people who don't perceive themselves as business angels and are therefore not members of business angel networks or other trade associations. Most of them don't advertise themselves as 'investors' but are interested in entrepreneurship and make early-stage investments just like other business angels.

Unlike members of business angel networks who have typically invested in five or 10 companies, new angels have maybe only invested in one or two. In most cases, they invest smaller sums than the other types of angels.

Despite the fact they invest in fewer deals and often with smaller sums, they are still a very important group of business angels for one simple reason: there are many more new angels than there are members of business angels' networks. If you aren't approaching new angels, you miss out on a good chance of securing funding for your startup.

You normally find these 'new angels' via your extended personal network. LinkedIn is a good starting point: look up people you know either directly or with mutual friends, who you know have money to invest (based upon their corporate career and/or own companies), and who you believe are interested in entrepreneurship (they have started or invested in other companies). New angels may be right under your nose, such as old classmates or a former boss.

Case study: I wish I had known this about business angels

Dan Eisenhardt, co-founder of Recon Instruments, explains:

We used business angels to fund the first few years at Recon Instruments. The vast majority of them were not part of any formal networks and none of them were famous or considered super angels. We found the angels via our extended networks, and they were often either successful entrepreneurs themselves or had successful corporate careers, and a common theme was a deep interest for startups and skiing.

Business angels don't invest because they like the PowerPoint and financial model you put together. They invest because they can connect with the idea, like you as a person, and believe you have what it takes to implement the solution you are selling to them.

Understanding these fundamental motivations helps you curate investor candidates, and once you have the right people selected you can focus on the in-person pitch more than the wordsmithing and graphics of the investor presentation. Those things are critical to get right as well, but on the day it all comes down to you as a founder.

Can you explain the value proposition in clear and concise terms? Can you articulate a strong vision and a believable story to get there? Can you continue to convince new

 © 2017 Nicolaj Højer Nielsen

investors to put money in to grow the business? Putting yourself in the angel investor's shoes, before presenting a pitch around these themes, will help you get them over the line.

How do you raise €200,000?

One challenge many founders face is that the amount they are looking to raise is more than an individual angel is capable of investing. This is most often the case with new angels, but most angels (whatever their type) typically invest less than €50,000 per round.

So how do you get your hands on the €200,000 you need?

You could chase the few big angels that have those funds, or you could go to business angel networks that syndicate funds. Most founders do this and overlook the third option – syndicating the investment themselves. Instead of asking one angel or angel network for €200,000, you get five angels to put in €40,000 each.

This syndication can also work to solve another classic problem with getting investors on board: the first angel is always the most difficult to land. Having the first on board will make it a lot easier to get the rest to sign – they're now more willing because they aren't the only one who thinks this is a good business opportunity.

Which angels should YOU start chasing?

With so many potential business angels – across all three types – that could all be interested in investing in your startup, which ones should you focus your attention on? I suggest you use the two main criteria for selecting the angels you should target, since these factors determine their likelihood-to-invest in a startup:

1. Angels who already know you
2. Angels who already know your industry

DOES THE BUSINESS ANGEL KNOW YOU?	Business angel doesn't know you at all	You're friend of a friend with a recommendation	The business angel ia a friend or relative who trusts you
The business angel has no clue about the industry			
The business angel has limited industry knowledge			
The business angel is an industry expert			

1. Angels who already know you

Early-stage investing is all about trust. At the early stage of development, you and the company don't have much to show. Maybe the product isn't even ready. Perhaps all you have is a few PowerPoint slides. Maybe you're still looking for key people to complete your team. And chances are you don't have any customers yet. All in all, your projections about future revenue and market size are crystal ball outlooks not verified by real customer data.

It takes a lot of trust on the part of a business angel to invest in such a company. They may accept that there's a real problem and your product is better at solving that problem than your competitors. What they worry about is you. Do you have what it takes to pull it off and beat the bad odds for early-stage startups where the vast majority fail? Personal trust is not something you build overnight.

In an ideal world, you would have already created trust with the investor through personal and/or professional relationships. That was the reason I invested in Recon Instruments. The co-founder and CEO, Dan Eisenhardt, is one of my close friends and I have the deepest respect for him personally and professionally. I didn't hesitate when he asked me to invest in his new company back in 2008.

In most cases, though, you won't be friends with the potential business angel. The next best alternative is to get a recommendation from a friend of a friend who can vouch for you. Look up the potential investor on LinkedIn, see if you have any mutual contacts and ask one of them to make an introduction. Note that this only works with people the angel actually trusts; second or third level connections aren't good enough.

2. Angels who already know your industry

The second important criterion is knowledge about the industry you are targeting.

Unlike VCs, angels often invest more or less alone. They don't have a team to help analyse the deal and the market. They depend on their own market knowledge and the information they get from their network of personal contacts.

If you're pitching a startup in an industry the angel understands, it's much more likely you will get a 'yes'. The angel either understands the problem you are solving directly or can confirm it by making a few phone calls. There is a good chance that this person will invest.

In the alternative scenario, where you are pitching a technology/industry the angel doesn't fully understand, it's very unlikely they will invest. They can't confirm your product is unique or validate that there aren't 20 other competitors doing exactly the same. The more technical/nerdy your innovation is, the harder it will be for outsiders to evaluate it. Chances are they have plenty of other investment opportunities they understand better and will simply decline your proposal and move on because they don't understand your business case in detail.

 © 2017 Nicolaj Højer Nielsen

The biggest mistake startups make when contacting angels:

Jesper Knudsen, partner at Accelerace (the startup accelerator), explains:

The biggest mistake I repeatedly see founders make is failing to understand the investors to whom they pitch. T hey fail to investigate what the investors know about the product/industry of their startups. The result is that the founders are totally unprepared when meeting the potential investor and therefore miss the opportunity to target their pitch to what that specific investor knows and is looking for.

I strongly advise founders to prioritise spending time to research the investor's background – including the investor's existing portfolio – before establishing contact. Actually, I always recommend you call a founder in one of the investor's portfolio companies to learn even more and maybe use them for a warm introduction – entrepreneurs tend to be willing to help each other. By doing your homework you get a much better understanding of whether your startup fundamentals meet the criteria/interest of the investor. At the end of the day, it's very unlikely the potential investor will decide to invest if they don't understand the space your startup is operating in, simply because they can't properly evaluate the risk/reward balance.

You as a founder should also carefully evaluate if you really want an investor who has no industry or domain knowledge since it's unlikely they'll be able to contribute knowhow or a network, and there's a risk they won't provide the expected value for you in the form of 'smart money '. Remember that on average a startup exists many years after receiving funding. Until the day of the great exit you will have to work closely with each other – through ups and downs – so pick your investors wisely.

 Key note: Spoiler: *Dragon's Den* isn't real!

Many first-time entrepreneurs base at least some of their knowledge of business angels on the popular TV show *Dragon's Den* (*Shark Tank* in the US and Australia). Here, a few entrepreneurs pitch their business ideas in front of a group of business angels (typically, famous super angels) who then – based on the pitch – decide if they want to invest or not.

It never works like this in the real world. Ever. Business angels need to evaluate not only the idea but also the people behind it and the traction (how far they've come); in other words, all that's needed to build the necessary trust in the business and founders, on which all angels build their investment decision. This can't be covered in 15 minutes. It makes great TV, but it's not real!

I am not suggesting the deals made on TV are fake – they are real, and it makes sense for the angels to do the deals on stage, given the huge publicity it gives them which more than pays for the additional risk of investing in unknown companies. But in the real world you can't get funding after a 15-minute meeting with the business angel!

What can angels offer you?

One of the big mistakes many entrepreneurs make when looking for business angel investors is only to look at the 'dilution' factor – how much equity the business angel investor will get, and how much cash they will pay for that.

The money/dilution is only one part of the equation when choosing from where to take your funding. You need to find out what the angel can and will do for your company, besides investing money.

Any business angel will claim you should accept their proposal because they bring in 'smart money'. That is, they not only come in with funding for your business, they will also help you succeed by providing experience, networks etc. This may well be true. If you choose the angel carefully, you will get both money and a person who has done it before, someone who is dedicated, and who can add more value – in other words, *smart money*.

 © 2017 Nicolaj Højer Nielsen

But let's be realistic. Just because you call yourself an angel or you have money doesn't mean you're smart. Even if you are smart, that doesn't mean you're willing to use that smartness on a weekly or regular basis in the service of the company. You could be dumb, you could have earned your money just by being lucky, or you could be involved in so many businesses you don't have time to help the startup on a regular basis.

 Key note: Do your homework on the angels!

One of the dangers for entrepreneurs is that angels promise a lot to startups to get the deal and then they don't deliver. You need to do your due diligence on the business angel before deciding who you want in your company – like the investors who check you out before they invest. Call some of the companies they have invested in and ask whether they keep their promises, add value, and do whatever they say they will do. If not, you need to question whether this is the right source of financing.

When you have checked them out, get on paper what you expect from them, both in terms of time dedication and specific tasks. Make an agreement about what will happen if they don't deliver on their part of the deal.

Take-away points

Most business angels are driven by more than money. If the only reward you offer is financial, you'll lose a lot of potential business angels. You need to understand what drives an angel and what you have to offer against what they're looking for. Look at what they've invested in the past.

Not even business angels invest in business *ideas*. You need to show you can do it and you've got what it takes to keep on doing it. So before you knock on the door, you need to get going yourself. Get a team and get working on converting your idea into a business.

Personal trust is one of the most important factors determining whether a business angel wants to invest. Look for angels who know you already, or who know the industry, because they'll be more comfortable analysing the risk/reward of your startup, even if they don't know who you are.

Do your homework and your due diligence. Call companies the angel has invested in. Did they get what was promised? Get all your agreements down on paper – including those not about money.

 © 2017 Nicolaj Højer Nielsen

© 2017 Nicolaj Højer Nielsen

Chapter 9:
Venture Capital

In this chapter you'll learn why venture capitalists are the biggest risk-takers and how they can afford to take those risks, why venture capitalists invest much later than most entrepreneurs think, and what venture capitalists are looking for. This will help you understand that most startups aren't suitable for venture capital and early stage startups are wasting their time chasing venture capital and should focus on getting their startup off the ground with bootstrapping and funding from other sources.

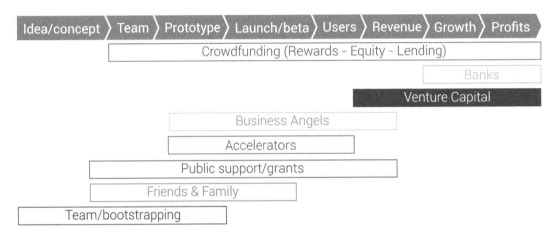

What is a VC fund?

A venture capital (VC) fund is an investment vehicle, typically created by a small group of people called the general partners. These general partners might be serial entrepreneurs who have some money that they want to invest in startups. However, they don't own the majority share of the fund; they have investors too.

Here is how VCs usually work: Typically three to five general partners come together to invest in a number of startups. They personally have €5 million to invest, but would really like to invest €100 million, so they go out to their investors and find the remaining €95 million. These millions are actually invested by people like you and me through the pension funds we contribute to each month. Pension funds don't invest in startups directly; they do so via VC funds.

Pension funds are so-called limited partners or sleeping partners in VC funds. They provide around 95 to 99 per cent of the capital, but are not involved in the day-to-day operations of the venture fund, which is handled entirely by the general partners who are responsible for the investment portfolio for each fund.

 © 2017 Nicolaj Højer Nielsen

Case study: CREANDUM - the birth of a venture fund

Creandum started in 2002 when Skandia and the Swedish National Pension Fund, two of the largest Swedish limited partners (LPs), decided to come together and start a seed stage venture fund for Sweden. To do so, they approached Staffan Helgesson who had become well known for running Start-up Factory (an investment company) and asked him if he would like to run the new fund as general partner (GP).

Helgesson brought in Stefan Lindeberg and Martin Hauge as fellow GPs to lead investments, as well as Fredrik Cassel (today a GP) as an investment analyst. They invested with mixed success in 10 companies in their first €30 million fund, following their investment mandate to focus on hardware and semiconductors.

In 2007 Creandum closed Fund II (€76 million), widening their scope to invest in 'the best tech-enabled entrepreneurs'. Creandum II appears as if it will be one of Europe's most successful early-stage funds, being the first institutional investor in category leaders like Spotify and iZettle. This success has enabled Creandum to successfully fundraise follow-up funds, with the Fund IV from 2015 (€180 million) as the largest and latest fund.

How do the general partners make their money?

These funds normally have a lifetime of 10 years. Funds typically only invest in startups for the first three years or so. The remaining seven years of the lifetime is used for reinvesting in existing startups in their portfolio and for hopefully selling (exiting) the companies to industrial buyers or bringing the companies to the stock-market (via an IPO).

Investment horizon for a VC fund

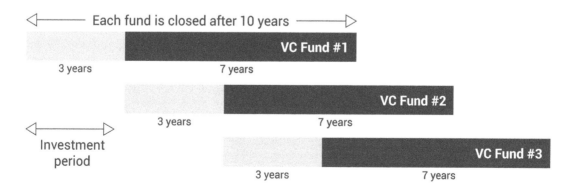

The general partners go to the pension funds every three or so years to make a new deal for a VC fund. This way, there are always funds coming to fruition and there is always money available to invest in new startups. If the general partners have been successful with the earlier funds, it will be easier for them to raise money from the pension fund investors for the subsequent VC fund.

 Key note: Is the VC fund actively investing?

It is important to check if the VC fund is in the active investing period before spending time on them. Check if they have raised a new fund within the last two or three years and also if they have actually invested in new companies lately. If not, then they are most likely in fundraising mode themselves and will not yet have fresh capital for investing in your startup. Thankfully, this is very easy to check, either via the media (including at industry sites such as Crunchbase or Pitchbook.VC) or the VC fund's own website, because all funds love to brag about both raising new funds and making new investments.

Why do the general partners create the funds in the first place?

As an entrepreneur out to raise money, it's crucial to understand what motivates VC fund general partners. Knowing how they think is key in understanding how to incentivise them to invest in your startup.

General partners make their money in two ways; management fees and carried interest.

Management fees

A management fee is typically two per cent per annum of the fund's capital, covering salaries for themselves, salaries for analysts and staff, administration costs and travel (for example). In the case of a fund with €100 million in capital, this management fee amounts to €2 million a year at a fee rate of two per cent.

Carried interest

However, the real reason they are involved in venture capital (at least in theory) is for the carried interest. Carried interest (carry) is a share of the profits of an investment or investment fund paid to the general partners in excess of the amount they contribute to the partnership. It is like a performance fee that rewards the general partners for their success in managing the fund.

 © 2017 Nicolaj Højer Nielsen

This carry is typically calculated as a share of the profits a fund makes, when the profit of the fund is higher than a certain hurdle rate (for example, eight per cent per annum). If the fund, when closed, has made less than this threshold in profit for the limited investors, the general partners get no bonus. However, for any profits above this threshold the general partners typically receive 20 per cent with the remaining 80 per cent going to the limited partners.

This can quickly become a very large sum of money to be shared by the general partners, best illustrated by the venture capital investment in WhatsApp, the largest VC-backed exit ever. The American VC fund Sequoia Capital invested $60 million in WhatsApp, which was then sold to Facebook for $16 billion. This gave the venture fund $3 billion in profit on this investment alone. Even when repaying the fund with interest to their investors, and assuming the unlikely scenario where all the other investments in the fund failed, the general partners of Sequoia most likely made hundreds of millions of dollars on this deal alone!

 Key note: Could you have the next WhatsApp?

The WhatsApp experience is what all venture capitalists dream of and think about when evaluating potential investments. Could this startup be the next WhatsApp / Instagram / Facebook / Google / Skype that will earn us millions in carried interest? If the partners don't believe your startup has this kind of potential (or at least an exit worth hundreds of millions of euros), then they are not that excited. Of course, they also know that this type of exit very rarely happens, but when making the initial investment they need to believe it could happen.

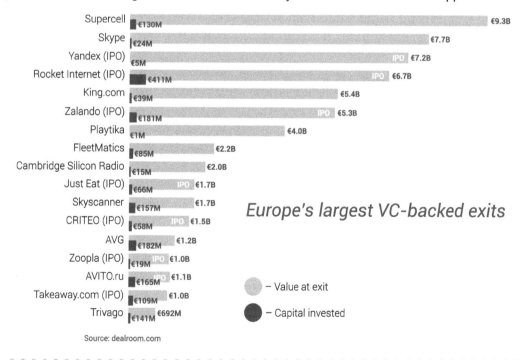

Europe's largest VC-backed exits

Source: dealroom.com

VC funds need to make it big

Entrepreneurs need to understand that general managers of VC funds are not interested in chasing exists in the €10 million range because of the compounded interest to be paid to the VC fund investors. The general partner will only get a big bonus if the fund returns significantly over the eight per cent compounded annual interest threshold to the investors. Say your goal as a fund is to make 15 per cent return per year; that might not sound much, but 15 per cent per annum over the ten-year period equals four times the invested amount. The VC fund general managers will need to return a ton of money to their investors to get their big bonuses!

If a VC fund of an initial €100 million is to be a success, the general managers will have to grow this to €400 million! And given that a VC fund normally only owns 20 to 30 per cent of the companies they invest in, the VC fund will have to invest in companies that are later sold/exited at €1-2 billion. And all this in less than 10 years!

Compound interest (10 years, 100 Million)

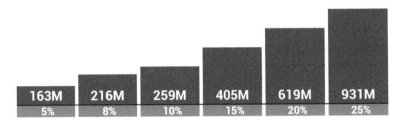

163M	216M	259M	405M	619M	931M
5%	8%	10%	15%	20%	25%

Key note: Rule of thumb – an investment should return half of the VC fund

The rule of thumb is that the potential return on an investment by a VC fund must equal half of the fund's size if the VC fund is to be interested. For a VC fund with €100 million in capital, the potential exit value for the VC must be €50+ million. But since the VC will normally own less than one third of the shares at exit, the company exit value will have to be in the €150+ million range to be interesting to a VC fund of this size.

How do venture capitalist funds invest?

There are several ways of making €100 million grow to €400 million in 10 years.

With the risk/reward matrix introduced earlier, you could either:

 © 2017 Nicolaj Højer Nielsen

1. Invest in companies that have a low risk of bankruptcy but at the same time don't have the high upside with the hope that the majority of the companies in the fund will improve in value by 10 to 15 per cent per annum and that the sum of this will return the fund several times (low risk/low reward strategy).

2. Invest in companies where many will fail but you hope that among the surviving ones there will be a few winners that will be able to return the fund multiple times (high risk/high reward strategy).

Venture Capital vs. Private Equity

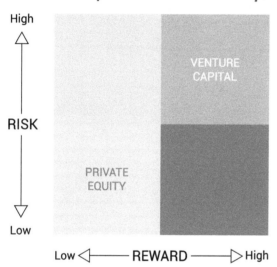

The above distinction is actually the difference between a private equity (PE) fund that invests in stable companies with low risk of bankruptcy, and a VC fund whose investment strategy is completely opposite. VC funds operate a high risk/high reward strategy. To be able to return €400 million to their investors, they are willing to take some wild bets. This is what venture capital is essentially about. They are positioned at the extreme end of the high risk/high reward matrix and are therefore only interested in startups that can become very big, very fast.

Why do 50% of all VC-backed startups fail?

This high risk/high reward strategy has one important implication for entrepreneurs. Most VC-backed startups are expected to fail or break even at best.

As seen in the illustration below, approximately 50 per cent of all deals that VCs invest in return less than the invested capital back to the VC fund (in popular terms called 'less than 1x'); a clear failure, most often resulting in the founder getting nothing or almost nothing when the company is closed. But the VC is willing to take such high risks because they are betting on the six per cent of all deals that return 10 times or more of the invested money. These few deals are responsible for 60 per cent of all returned capital to the VC!

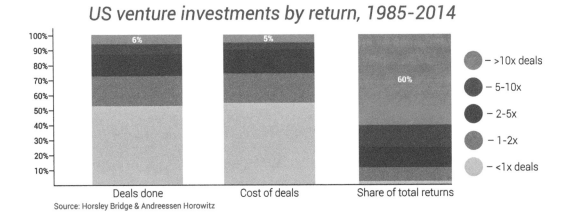

US venture investments by return, 1985-2014

Source: Horsley Bridge & Andreessen Horowitz

* *

(!) **Key note: 10X**

Every VC knows that it's the very few big exits that will determine the success of the fund. There is therefore a rule of thumb that you can only get the VC interested in a potential deal if they hope there is at least a chance that the potential investment will return more than 10 times the invested money!

* *

A second, and even more important, point is to decide if you are willing to take the risk that goes with having VC funds as investors. Why do 50 per cent of all venture capital-backed startups fail? Part of the reason is that they are immature, early in the market and very new, and because of all this they are high risk. But more importantly it is because of the high-risk strategies that the venture capitalists want startups to follow. Since the venture capital funds are only looking for big exits, this means that they often 'force' the startup to chase a 'winner takes all' strategy. This might create a huge profit if it succeeds, but the chance of it doing this is very slim. A classic example might be a software company that has reached some sort of success in a local market. This might not create a billion euro company, but now the company has to decide – should they try to scale their business at a global level (with the high risk and high reward as a result) or should they focus on consolidating their business locally? If you have a VC on board in your company, I know which direction they will fight for. Entrepreneurs need to ask themselves if they are willing to commit to those strategies and the 50 / 50 chance of going bankrupt that goes with them.

 © 2017 Nicolaj Højer Nielsen

Or as Kasper Brandi Pedersen, co-founder of The Cloakroom, explains:

"VCs are not your friends. They are your business partners and they care about all their investments. But they only need to be successful with one out of 10 startups while you as a founder prefer to be successful with one out of one startups you build."

"This creates some interesting dynamics that are helpful, but also dangerous. We typically saw our investors pushing for faster growth and higher burn, and as aggressive young entrepreneurs we went for it. In hindsight, a more sustainable growth would have enabled us to fix fires with real solutions instead of sticking plasters."

VC funding too early is bad for your startup

Most entrepreneurs believe that the lack of funding is one of the main reasons startups don't succeed. This might be true, but studies suggest the opposite is also a risk: too much funding too early in the startup's life can lead to failure.

In Startup Genome's analysis of 3200 high-tech startups, they concluded that 70% of those that failed did so NOT because of lack of experience among founders, lack of funding or other commonly accepted risk factors, but what they called "premature scaling". This can be defined as growing your company/organisation and spending too much money on development, marketing or other costs before you have a product that sufficiently satisfies your customers' needs. In startup jargon, this point is called "product/market fit". Reaching product/market fit tends to take a much longer time than the founders initially expect, leading to many iterations before you nail it, and have a product your customers actually want to use and pay for.

So what happens if you expand your organisation before reaching this point? Your startup becomes less flexible, because you have a much bigger ship to steer. You can't simply switch your focus from product X to product Y if you have 30 people on your team and have already launched a big marketing campaign for product X. This is possible with 3-4 co-founders and a smaller market, but not when you grow. The limited flexibility reduces the chances of you perfecting your product for your customers, thereby increasing the chances your startup will die.

But what has premature scaling to do with venture capital? Premature scaling costs money and, as you are doing it before you receive a lot of revenue from your customers, it is normally paid for by external investors. Business angel funding tends to be in smaller rounds, thereby reducing the risk of premature scaling compared to the larger investments venture capital provides. Or as venture capitalist Michael A. Jackson explains in the Startup Genome report:

"Venture-backed startups have no option but to scale eventually. Investors have made their investment based on the fact that they believe the startup is a scalable business that can attack a large market. Getting venture money can be like putting a rocket engine on the back of a car. Scaling comes down to making sure the machine is ready to handle the speed before hitting the accelerator."

Case Study: Premature Scaling at Addwish

Background: Addwish was initially a wish list solution for consumers and online stores that allowed users to manage the registration and purchase of gifts. The company was started by Brian Petersen and Kasper Refskou Jensen as a side project, which both worked on part-time. The two co-founders had managed to sign up a hundred web shops and had a total of 20,000 users who had tried their service. In early 2013 the company received a €1.5 million seed investment from venture capital fund Sunstone. Now the goal became to do an international rollout – very fast.

Kasper Refskou explains:

"For the first year we had a goal of one million consumers on the wish list – a 50-fold increase! This meant a fast ramp-up from two part-time employees to 12 full-time employees during Christmas 2013. We also started to spend heavily on marketing, including some heavy Adwords campaigns for user acquisitions in the US. This led to a sharp increase in burn-rates, which rose to €100,000 a month. The initial strategy was to build a critical mass of consumers (who use the wish lists for free), and then monetize on the web-shops."

"We just didn't manage to reach those figures. For the first year we got 100,000 consumers – a huge growth, but only 10% of projections. So since the revenue stream from the web shops was still not in effect, this slower-than-anticipated growth was critical."

"But the worst part was that we didn't recognize until way too late we were heading in the wrong direction. We had lost our objectivity during the rush for the Christmas season peak. Despite so many clear signals of low traction in the consumer market and being unable to achieve the key performance, we didn't realize we were dying until we were actually dead! We woke up way too late, when we had only just made the initial entry into selling and revenue generation, resulting in the company being on the brink of bankruptcy by January 2015."

"I guess this is what happens when two inexperienced entrepreneurs receive too much unrestricted funding. With too little guidance and supervision, we entered into a-way-too-high burn rate resulting in only one option: go big or go bankrupt."

"In perfect hindsight, it's easy to see what went wrong: we started scaling before we had reached a product-market fit. A wish list did not have a viral loop that was fast

 © 2017 Nicolaj Højer Nielsen

enough to meet our goals. When you share something on Facebook it triggers the recipients to share it again straight away. But when you share a wish list, the recipient may like the product, but they don't need to create their own birthday wish list at that exact moment, which is why the sharing and viral metrics take a lot longer. We were blind to this at that time. If we had noticed it in earlier, we could have changed strategy before it was too late."

Unlike most cases of premature scaling, this one ended well. Before going bankrupt, the venture capital fund sold its shares to a local business angel, Niels Henrik Rasmussen, who injected more capital into the company to keep it afloat. Admirably, the VC initiated and supported these changes in order to help the business survive.

With the new owner also came a new and improved turn-around strategy, now focused on building the B2B segment first. The company was able to become early-stage positive within seven months due to a rapidly growing customer base of 400+ e-commerce businesses.

Kasper Refskou elaborates:

"Our turnaround made us focus on what we did really well: approaching the business segment (web shops), and making use of the technology that brings them higher conversion rates and larger basket size. If we were to do it all again, we would do it very much like we do today: "identify – test – adjust".

Perhaps what you think is a goldmine, might not be. It's essential to test out every initiative, being truly honest with yourself about the results. It may not be a bad idea, but perhaps the audience is not ready for it, the tech is not there yet or the adoption triggers are not present. But get the right people and make sure they see the vision as you do, and you will eventually find a way. Now that we are mainly focusing on the B2B segment, it's quite funny to see that our wish list, two years after our big launch and missed KPIs, has gotten more air beneath its wings. This time, without any marketing-related initiatives, we can see that the 100,000 users have more than tripled, and that social sharing is slowly becoming our main acquisition channel for wish list users. Now we have also included the wish list data in our intelligent data analysis for even better personalization in our business offering. In some ways you can say that we have gone full circle – just the other way around."

What do VC funds invest in?

Now you know more about how VC funds make their money and what sort of return on investment they need to be successful, let's look at the types of startups VC funds actually invest in. In short, a VC is looking for a startup that has a:

1. Much better product
2. Scalable business
3. Huge market

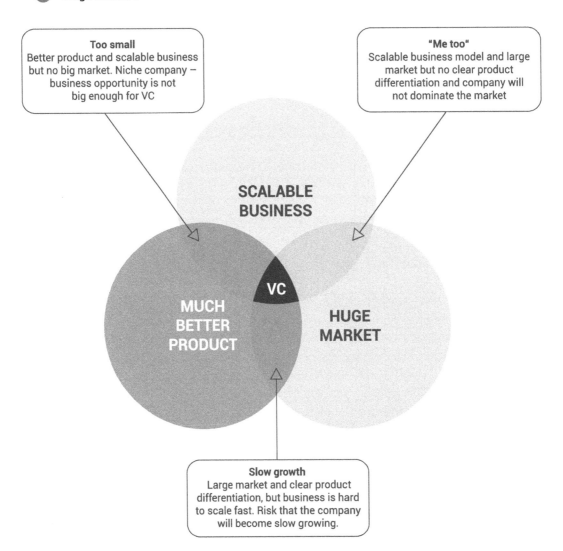

Too small
Better product and scalable business but no big market. Niche company – business opportunity is not big enough for VC

"Me too"
Scalable business model and large market but no clear product differentiation and company will not dominate the market

Slow growth
Large market and clear product differentiation, but business is hard to scale fast. Risk that the company will become slow growing.

SCALABLE BUSINESS

VC

MUCH BETTER PRODUCT

HUGE MARKET

 © 2017 Nicolaj Højer Nielsen

1. Much better product

To be interesting to a VC fund, your company's product has to be much better than the offerings from existing companies. Not just 10 per cent better than existing products, but 10 times better.

This is because VCs are only interested in investments that can grow 10-fold in value in just a few years. For this to be possible, the new startup has to be able to gain a large market share. And if you are only 10 per cent better than existing big players and/or other startups, that is simply not realistic.

Example	"Incremental innovation" – not that interesting for VCs	"10X better" – very interesting for VCs
Consumer electronics / gadgets	A new smart watch, with more functionality than existing products	A new class of gadgets / electronics, e.g. computers integrated into the human body/brain
Software	A customer relationship management (CRM) system with a better user interface than the market leaders	A CRM system using machine learning to automatically input data, to replace human entries
Energy storage	A battery type that is 10% more compact that existing ones	Storing energy in completely different ways from today to gain 10-fold benefits (e.g. Tesla Powerwall)

What you have to offer a VC fund must be revolutionary. Startups are at an initial disadvantage in terms of distribution, brand etc. compared with existing companies. VC funds are looking for something that will revolutionise the industry because the product is much better or the way you bring it to the market is much better.

Being 10 times better leads into the next point; you need to have a scalable business.

2. Scalable business

VC funds not only need to make a lot of money for their investors – they need to do so very quickly. Because the life cycle time of a VC fund is typically 10 years, the fund will need to exit from the business in less than five years. And in those five years the value of the company will need to grow 10, 20 or 30-fold.

Some industries and products are simply much easier to grow (scale) quickly and remain cost-efficient than others. A social media platform is one example of a very scalable business able to grow to millions of users very quickly.

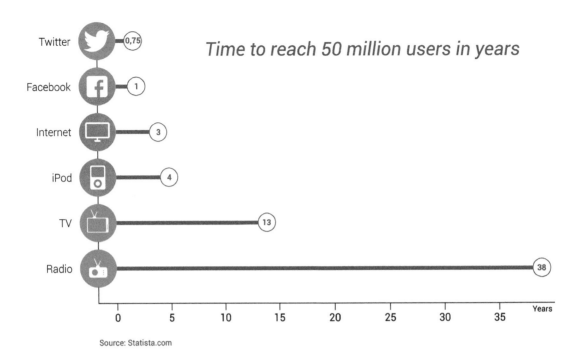

Time to reach 50 million users in years

Source: Statista.com

Businesses that allow a successful company to grow fast are typically characterised by a high degree of automation, and don't involve much physical labour. Examples are software and medicine. In a software company, you develop the product, which might be very expensive, but your production and distribution cost will be very low and you can add more customers at a relatively low cost. In medicine you develop the drug, which costs billions of dollars and is very high risk, but when you have it approved in one market you can sell it in many more markets very quickly, with very high margins since your production costs are low.

Businesses which are difficult to scale are those which are human or capital asset intensive, such as consulting companies or restaurants. Let's say you've developed the best restaurant in the world; the question is how fast can you grow and become a billion-euro business? To do so you need to build more restaurants and hire and train thousands of employees. All of this takes time, and it requires a lot of cash to cover capital expenditure and operational costs. Restaurants are therefore not very scalable businesses. Even with its franchise business model, it took McDonalds 20 years to reach $1 billion in revenue! This is way too slow for a VC, considering that the total lifetime of the VC fund is normally 10 years.

In comparison, it took Facebook approximately five years to reach $1 billion in revenue.

Not only does the project have to be much better, the business also has to be highly scalable if VC funds are to be interested. But that is still not enough; for those two factors to make sense for the VC, the market size also has to be big enough.

 © 2017 Nicolaj Højer Nielsen

3. Large market

What a VC fund is even more adverse to than a failing company is a situation where a company turns out to be successful but the market it operates in turns out to be too small to rapidly build a highly valuable company.

In most markets, even the leading player will not have a global market share that is higher than 10 to 20 per cent. Of course there are the few 'Googles', who basically own an industry (web search) with a 50 per cent-plus market share, but in most industries this is not the case.

If the market turns out to be too small, and the startup company 'only' gets (say) 10 per cent of the market, there is a high risk that the company doesn't fit the VC criteria in terms of value. The reverse calculation the VC fund makes goes like this:

Fifteen million euros in exit value would be satisfactory to most entrepreneurs, but is far less than needed to make most VC funds interested.

In other words, given the above assumptions, a €100 million market is too small for most venture capitalists! The rule of thumb is that it has to be a 'several hundred million euro market' for the smaller VC funds to be interested. And a 'billion euro market' before you might have a venture capital case for a large VC fund, since it takes very large markets to make the potential exit value big enough for venture capital scale.

Case Study: The Cloakroom — good for angels, too small for VCs

Background: The Cloakroom is the previously mentioned e-commerce startup focusing on online personal shopping for men. Co-founder Kasper Brandi explains how venture capital funds perceived the investment case compared to how business angels looked at it:

E-commerce is less interesting for VCs because the prospect of you outperforming the large incumbent companies (like Amazon) is tiny. But the risk is also considerably lower than in many other cases since there are a lot of online and offline retailers who are potential acquirers. These guys are now so hungry to join the e-commerce train that they accept higher valuations than ever before. It's low risk and low reward from the VC point of view.

Angels are less turned off, though. They might be excited about the potential of building a decent €20+ million niche business and being acquired by Zalando or Amazon, even though the potential return on investment is not large enough to satisfy a traditional VC.

 Key note: Don't waste time pitching non-VC cases

Don't waste time preparing a pitch to a VC for a startup business that isn't much better than the alternatives, isn't highly scalable, and/or doesn't address a large market. No matter how good your project is, it isn't a VC case and you won't be successful in selling it to a VC fund.

How many startups qualify for VC funding?

By now you are hopefully asking yourself, does my company fit what venture capital funds will be interested in investing in? The answer is most likely 'no'. Only a fraction of companies are relevant for venture capital and they are the anomalies, the freaks, and the outliers.

Let's look at the statistics globally, across all types of venture capital, from the earliest invest-ment round to very large stage deals. In 2015, 8,000 companies received $129 billion in ven-ture funding.

Venture capital funding per year

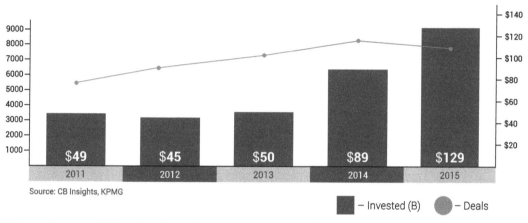

Source: CB Insights, KPMG

⬛ – Invested (B)　⬤ – Deals

This might sound like a lot, but when compared with the total number of new companies out there, it isn't. There are more than 100 million companies in the world. Assuming a company lives on average for 10 years, this means that 10 million new companies are created globally per year. But only 8,000 of those receive VC funding. In other words, approximately only 0.1% of all new companies receive funding from venture capital. Even in industries that VC funds are actively looking to invest in (IT, life sciences, and clean tech), only a very small fraction of the new companies is funded by venture capital.

Case study: Recon Instruments - I wish I had known this about venture capital funds when I started

Dan Eisenhardt, co-founder of Recon In-struments, explains:

I wish I had known that VC funds act in al-most the opposite way to business angels. They are very critical about the plan and the numbers upfront. Here a poorly put togeth-er investor package will certainly disquali-fy you from 90 per cent of VCs, even if you have a strong pitch and appealing person-ality, because you won't even get the first meeting.

A VC doesn't have to connect with your idea as a user, but they do need to see your company fit into a larger story about what's hot in the macro environment. Understanding how you fit into a broader vision or trend in the market with clear company comparables is a necessity to get a VC to come onto your side and listen to your pitch. It will also help you identify the VCs that would be able to help you grow your business, as VCs typically invest according to pre-set themes, industry focus and stage of growth. Once you have a check mark next to the plan and the 'where you fit into this world', the same principles apply in terms of you as a founder, but you need to pass those gates first.

Understanding this from the onset would have saved me a lot of time and it would have made me much more focused and diligent with my plan and identifying our fit within broader industry trends before approaching VCs.

When do venture capitalists invest?

If you still think your project is a candidate for VC funding, you need to find out when is the right time to approach them. Venture capitalists don't invest as early as many entrepreneurs think. This is for two reasons:

1. VCs, like other professional investors, are cynical about the value of a business idea. At the idea stage it's simply impossible to judge whether the startup has venture potential (much better product + scalable business + large market) or not. VCs know the hard part is not coming up with the initial idea, but the actions taken AFTER the idea conception. And that part — the progress/traction — takes time to prove. Even if you have VC funding potential, the funds will only invest *after* you have set the team, built the first product, and (in many cases) already begun selling your product. The capital needed to reach that point will have to be secured from other sources.

2. The second reason VC funds invest later than entrepreneurs think is because VC funds would rather invest €5 million than €50,000 in a startup. VC funds are normally managed by a small number of general partners who not only have to source new deals, but also participate at board level (and even at an operational level) in the companies they invest in. It is simply not possible for a €100 million fund to divide that capital into 200 different companies. The due diligence process and legal paperwork for 200 investments will be very demanding and expensive to handle, and it will be impossible for the five partners to each sit on the board of 40 or so companies. VC funds normally invest a large amount in only in a limited number of companies per fund (typically around 20).

 © 2017 Nicolaj Højer Nielsen

Key note: It's hard to get a 'no' from a VC

The only thing harder than getting a YES from a VC is getting a NO. Peecho's experience illustrates this point perfectly; they launched their concept at TheNextWeb Conference in 2010 with no orders and no customers. But to give an example of the platform and what it could offer, they had created a small application on top of the platform – a mobile app for sending postcards. This idea turned out to fall within the likes of the conference competition jury and Peecho won first prize within the category of 'most promising business model'. It created a lot of media attention and investors started to flock to Peecho. Sander Nagtegaal explains:

VCs in general are very nice and clever people. They will always be nice to you because they never know how successful 'this guy' is going to be later. So in the end you have lots of talks, which is useful because they [VCs] are smart and can help you, however, this takes a lot of time if you have to travel around the world. We talked to all of them and they all said the same thing – eventually. It was always like a long no and they always said: 'We need more traction – you're just not big enough yet'.

Peecho ended up wasting a lot of time talking with VCs when it was way too early for VCs to invest in them. But it's really hard to get a real NO from a VC because they want to be friendly to you just in case you turn out to be the next Facebook!

Finding the right VC fund

If VC funding is right for your startup, your next step is to find the right fund; one that is investing in startups at the stage yours is in and is in your country.

1. The right stage

Not only do VC funds invest much later than most entrepreneurs think, they are also a very diverse group of investors who invest in very different stages of the company. Typically, only a fraction of VC funds are relevant for early-stage entrepreneurs.

The difference in when the different types of VC funds invest, and how much, is illustrated below:

INVESTMENT SIZE	FUNDING STAGE	VENTURE INVESTORS
€10K–€500K	**Pre-seed** Prove the idea is worth exploring	Too early for VC
€1–2M	**Seed round** Prove the business model is working	Seed funds, Small VC funds
€2–10M	**Series A** Prove you can scale the startup	Large VC funds
+ €10M	**Series B, C etc** Prove the company can become the (global) market leader	Large VC funds, Traditional PE

After you have reached the point of being VC funding ready, and have demonstrated that you, your product, and the market for that product all have what it takes to be of interest to a VC fund, you need to identify the VCs who might be interested in investing in your startup. These particular VCs are the so-called 'early-stage funds'.

The first round of venture capital in a company is often called 'Series A', referring to the first round of preferred stock these investors normally get for their investment. These Series A investment rounds are typically €2-5 million in Europe, but differ significantly from company to company. A few of the early-stage rounds even invest a bit earlier than the classic Series A, called a 'seed round'. These investments are typically in the €1-2 million range for each company they invest in.

For an entrepreneur looking for initial venture capital, it is therefore very important to focus attention only on these early-stage funds who are investing in seed and Series A, and *not* on all the other venture funds who invest in later stages, and who will therefore never consider investing 'only €1-2 million' in your company. They are all looking for investment opportunities that are much more mature. The rule of thumb is the bigger the fund, the later they invest.

 Key note: Finding VC funds in the right stage

The quickest way to check is to visit the VC fund websites. Most will tell which stages the particular fund invests in, which together with information on their previous investments gives you a clear sign of whether they are interesting for you or not. If their last 10 investments have been €50 or €100 million, the chance they will invest €2 million in your project is virtually non-existent.

 © 2017 Nicolaj Højer Nielsen

1. **SEED STAGE:** Typically this is, when you have a product, and you have a great team. However, you might have a beta version on the market with a few users, but you don't really have that much data in support of your business potential. You think your business could become very big and you need €1 million to prove it. Let's say your prototype car has four wooden wheels and a really small engine you have taken from a scooter and now you need to show that it can actually run. What you need is a bit of petrol to prove it.

2. **SERIES A:** You have the product working, you have a strong team, you have happy customers, and you have real revenue, or if you are in the consumer software business (where initial products tend to be free), you have a user base that is growing at an exponential rate with very limited marketing costs. What you need is the capital necessary for growing the business, typically in the form of much higher spending on sales and marketing. You will typically raise €2-5 million. You have a small engine and you, your co-driver, and a few passengers are driving around in your small car and it sort of works. What you need is a bigger engine, more fuel, and to fix all those little things that don't quite work yet.

3. **LATE STAGE/GROWTH:** In the late stage scenario, you would be a global leader wanting to raise €10-100 million. You won't raise this amount of money for something that isn't working. In the early stage you were building the car, and now you want the car to be on the road in every single country in the world. You raise the money to build a car factory for a car that already works.

Case study: Trustpilot – from idea to venture capital funding

The Trustpilot case study contains many of the key take-aways with regards to venture capital funding – that the VC is almost never the first investor and that when VCs invest, the local funds invest first and then, when you have to scale internationally, syndicates with a larger and more international VCs step in.

In 2006, Peter Mühlmann, then a student from Aarhus, Denmark had an idea: he wanted to create transparency in online shopping and reduce fraud through a platform driven by customer reviews – reviews that could be trusted.

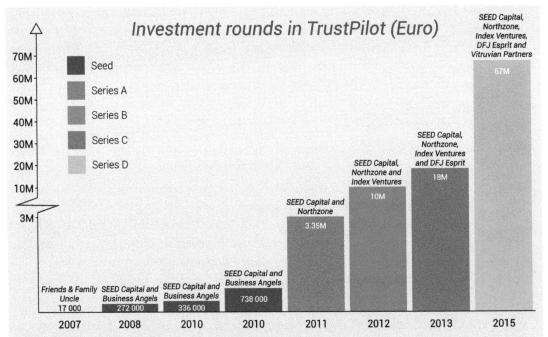

Investment rounds in TrustPilot (Euro)

Legend	
Seed	Series A
Series B	Series C
Series D	

Year	Investors	Amount
2007	Friends & Family Uncle	17 000
2008	SEED Capital and Business Angels	272 000
2010	SEED Capital and Business Angels	336 000
2010	SEED Capital and Business Angels	738 000
2011	SEED Capital and Northzone	3.35M
2012	SEED Capital, Northzone and Index Ventures	10M
2013	SEED Capital, Northzone, Index Ventures and DFJ Esprit	18M
2015	SEED Capital, Northzone, Index Ventures, DFJ Esprit and Vitruvian Partners	67M

In 2007, the idea turned into reality: Peter founded Trustpilot, an online review community that made it possible for consumers to read and write reviews. Peter happened to have a wealthy uncle who he told about his idea and asked him for €130,000. Peter's uncle gave him €17,000 in exchange for equity in Trustpilot.

In 2008, Trustpilot got their first seed investment from Danish early-stage VC SEED Capital, followed by further capital injection in 2010. Lars Andersen, general partner in SEED Capital, explains:

Peter had, with his idea about user-generated content and peer-to-peer reviews, tapped directly into two hot trends. Here was a case which had enormous growth potential and an uncontested market. Peter had market traction but still needed to find the recipe for a sustainable business model.

Once Trustpilot zeroed in on the right business model, a pivotal moment occurred: new business customers began actively encouraging their customers to review their purchase on Trustpilot, which resulted in more new business customers. The amount of incoming reviews soared and Trustpilot took off.

By the summer of 2010, Trustpilot had grown from a small startup to a fully fledged organisation. In December that year Peter and his investors started looking for additional funding to secure future growth and scale the company across Europe. After pitching to numerous investors, Peter had the rare pleasure of holding term sheets from five different investors in his hands. In the end, Northzone was chosen as syndication partner, which resulted in a €3.4 million series A investment in 2011. A year later, Peter once

 © 2017 Nicolaj Højer Nielsen

again found himself holding competing term sheets, which resulted in Index Ventures joining Trustpilot's investor team with a €10 million series B investment.

By 2013, Trustpilot had built a strong European base, employing 160 people. The time had come to approach the American market. The years 2014 and 2015 brought both series C and D investments, bringing venture funds Draper Esprit and Vitruvian Partners on board, along with a total of €90 million to further fund the Trustpilot journey. And as Peter mentioned after the new round was announced: *You're not getting €90 million to do something new. You're getting the money to do more of what you're already doing.*

2. In the right industry (and partner)

Not only do most VC funds specialise in investments in companies at specific stages of development, they often also tend to specialise in certain industries.

European VC rounds by sector in 2015

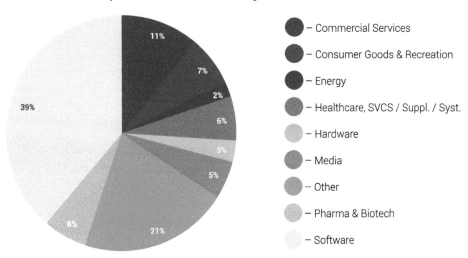

Source: Pitchbook.

VC funds invest in a broad range of sectors, as illustrated above – everything from drug development and consumer hardware to internet based services. But most funds specialise in a few specific sectors and won't be interested in cases outside their specialties, where they have built up unique business and market knowledge which increases their chances of picking the right investments.

The first task of the entrepreneur is therefore to identify VC funds which invest in the business you are in. Again, this is relatively easy to find on their websites.

Key note to entrepreneurs: Target the right VC partner

Next comes a crucial step that many entrepreneurs overlook: you need to identify and target the right partner within the fund. Think about it this way: imagine a fund dedicated to IT – a relatively broad sector that covers business-to-business software, IT-security, mobile games, and maybe even consumer hardware. The three to 10 partners each have their business specialities. When researching the fund, find out which general partner within the fund is in charge of investments that look the most like yours. This person is most likely the right person for you, and by targeting that person you improve your chances of the fund taking a closer look at your investment proposal.

3. In the right geographical location!

One of the most common mistakes made by European startups looking for VC funding is to travel to Sand Hill Road in Silicon Valley, south of San Francisco. This is the address where most of the leading US VC funds have their headquarters. European entrepreneurs go there in the hope of securing capital for their startups.

Most of them are welcomed and get to meet the VCs. Very few – including those with the funding cases best suited for VC funding – get funding. Why? For three reasons:

1. **Legal.** Most of these investment funds have an 'investment mandate' from their investors to invest only in North American companies. So, unless the European startup moves to the US, the VC fund will not be allowed to invest.

2. **Proximity.** A VC fund will normally take a seat on the board of your company. They are not going to want, nor will they have the time, to fly around Europe to meetings with portfolio companies. The fact is that many of the local VCs at Sand Hill Road prefer investing in companies in 'the valley'.

3. **Trust.** VC funding is high risk, and all VCs know that success relies on the people making up the company. VCs invest in people they trust – preferably people they know already, or who come with strong recommendations from mutual connections. If you're from Europe, chances are the VCs don't know you and therefore the likelihood of them trusting you enough to invest in your team is slim.

This is especially true for early-stage investments where the investment sums are smaller (and not worth travelling long distances for), and the risk is very high (lack of data to prove your case if they don't know you).

Unless you and your team actually have a real desire to move your company to California (not

 © 2017 Nicolaj Højer Nielsen

only formally, but actually relocating the management team there), you will be wasting your time by trying to book meetings with VC funds based in Silicon Valley.

Key note to entrepreneurs: Focus initially on local VC funds

Focus on VC funds closer to you, preferably in your country but at least in the same region (for example, some London-based VCs invest across Europe, but it's unthinkable that the same partner would invest in an early-stage startup located in South-East Asia, unless the VC has an office in that region). Local VC funds are the ones most likely to invest in your company. However if they invest when your startup needs more money to scale further, it might be relevant to target larger funds located elsewhere who might want to co-invest in your company together with the locally based fund.

Case Study: Silicon Valley VC funds invest in local startups

Shomit Ghose is a general partner at a Silicon Valley venture capital fund, Onset Ventures, which invests in early-stage software companies. Prior to becoming a VC he was an entrepreneur and part of three successful IPOs. He explains how Silicon Valley VCs are different and why they prefer to invest locally:

From an investor standpoint, the key thing that Silicon Valley has that's unique in the world is a set of risk-willing VCs who were all entrepreneurs themselves in the past. They see an early-stage startup not as pure risk, as VCs elsewhere might, but as an opportunity. Silicon Valley VCs are very familiar and comfortable with the work required to make a startup successful. They know you don't reduce startup risk by simply exacting aggressive financing terms from an early-stage company; the only thing that reduces startup risk is excellence in execution. Silicon Valley VCs focus on providing value by drawing on their own experience as entrepreneurs and act as operators to help guide startups to excellence in execution.

Because investors can only reduce the risk in an early-stage startup by giving it guidance and operational help, Silicon Valley VCs prefer that the startups be based in Silicon Valley as well. It's impossible to give an early-stage startup the help it needs from 5000 miles away. So if you're an early-stage deal, and want to raise money from Silicon Valley VCs, you should plan on having your management team based in Silicon Valley.

Investment decision process at a VC fund

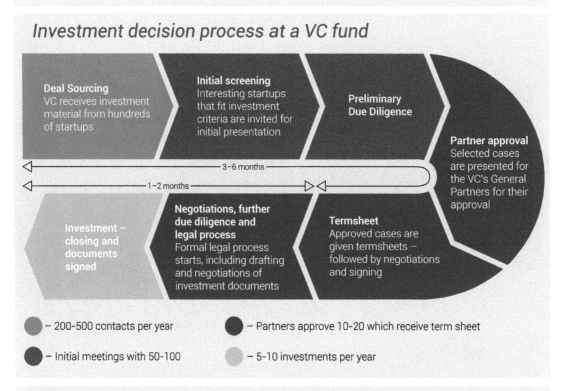

Deal Sourcing
VC receives investment material from hundreds of startups

Initial screening
Interesting startups that fit investment criteria are invited for initial presentation

Preliminary Due Diligence

Partner approval
Selected cases are presented for the VC's General Partners for their approval

3–6 months

1–2 months

Investment – closing and documents signed

Negotiations, further due diligence and legal process
Formal legal process starts, including drafting and negotiations of investment documents

Termsheet
Approved cases are given termsheets – followed by negotiations and signing

- 200-500 contacts per year

- Partners approve 10-20 which receive term sheet

- Initial meetings with 50-100

- 5-10 investments per year

VC: You need to sell all the way to the end!

One of the classic mistakes startups make when searching for VC money is to feel certain that the money is secured before the process is complete. But as statistics show, you must keep selling until an offer is made! Or as Christian Thaler-Wolski explains from his experience as a venture capitalist:

Once I invited a company to the partner meeting, we were already convinced the startup's team, market and technology were great. The final meeting was to make sure everyone had met the team and it withstood

 © 2017 Nicolaj Højer Nielsen

the scrutiny of the firm's four partners. After that we would issue a term sheet and move into formal due diligence. The teams that didn't make that final cut almost always made one mistake: they thought they had it bagged. Believing they were 95 per cent home and the last presentation was just a formality, they lacked energy, their answers to our questions conflicted with those given at previous meetings, and sometimes they were 'too honest'. Remember, you are selling until the last second and, just like everyone else, investors want to be sold to.

What do venture capitalists want in return?

The one question all startups ask is how much the VC funds want in return for an investment. Some entrepreneurs mistakenly believe that a venture capitalist wants it all. Not the case. They typically only want a stake of between 20 and 49 per cent, for two reasons:

1. They're not running your company
2. VCs want the core team to have enough equity to go for more funding rounds

The rule of thumb is that each venture run will cost you 20 to 30 per cent of your business. But typically a startup that receives VC funding doesn't stick to one round of financing. Typically, you get several rounds involving different VCs – each wanting 20 to 30 per cent. So in total the VCs often have the majority of the shares when the company is exited.

The VC is in control - use a good lawyer!

Most first-time entrepreneurs believe control of your company is about owning 51 per cent of the shares. Nothing could be more wrong, especially if your minority shareholders are venture capital funds!

How do they do it? Typically by implementing different measures into the associations of the company and in the shareholders' agreements in the form of technical terms like 'preference shares', 'board control', 'veto rights', 'key man clauses' etc. These things allow the VC (even though they own less than 50 per cent of the shares) to enforce things like firing the CEO (you!), changing the strategy of your company, and controlling when and how shares in the company can be sold and new equity be taken in. Firing a founder who is a CEO of the company is actually a quite standard practice of professional investors, with Steve Jobs fired as CEO of Apple as the most famous example.

Is it bad for the company that the VC is in control? Not necessarily. They don't plan to fire the CEO when they initially invest in a startup because they typically invest in the team. But, if things don't go as planned, the VC always reserve the right to do so!

So if you consider taking VC funds in as investors, you need to know what you're getting into.

If you're not an expert in venture financing, you need to team up with a good lawyer who is experienced in dealing with VCs so they can advise you on the consequences of the proposed VC investment and start negotiating terms!

Advice from a VC: We want the entrepreneur to be driven by more than money

Jimmy Fussing Nielsen is managing partner at Sunstone Capital and explains why being driven by money is not enough to convince a VC to invest in your startup:

It can sound like a cliché, but as a venture capital investor I want to invest in founders who are passionate about what they are doing and want to create some kind of change in the world. I firmly believe the best founders are driven by a strong vision and not only by financial gain. I believe this view is shared by most VC investors.

So why do we want them to be driven by more than money? Isn't that a paradox, given that the venture capital fund itself is created to provide financial return to our investors, our limited partners? The reason is simple. We know how hard it is to create a successful startup and how long a time and how many ups and downs it takes before you make it! If you are only driven by financial gain when dealing with all these crises, it will be very hard for you to keep up the positive spirit. And it will be even harder for you to attract the human talent needed to make your startup a success. People want to work for founders who have a bigger cause than just making money. And VCs want to invest in such founders!

Take-away points

Venture capital is not for everyone. Very few companies fit the criteria for venture capital investment. You have to be unique – a freak, actually. You need a much better product or offering, in a highly scalable industry, in a very large market. Not many startups qualify for this, and only a very small fraction of startups are financed by venture capital.

But even if your startup could get investment from a venture capital fund, you should think

 © 2017 Nicolaj Højer Nielsen

twice before actually doing it. Taking venture capital will lead to a "go big or go bankrupt" strategy since venture capital funds are only interested in companies that go after exits in the €100 million-plus range. Such "high reward" strategies come with high risks, which venture capital funds and their managers are happy to take because they only need 1-2 of the 20 startups in the fund to succeed. But are you willing to take the risk of being among the many VC-backed startups that go bankrupt?

VCs are willing to take very high risks, but invest much later than you think. Don't go to a venture capitalist hoping they will become your first investor; they won't. A venture capital investment is possible only after you have already proved the business potential, and this normally comes after other types of investors (angels, accelerators, and friends) have already put money into the company.

Early-stage venture capital is extremely local. If you've contacted big American funds who only have headquarters in Silicon Valley and you're located in London, they will most likely not invest. So if it's venture capital you're after, you will have to target the right funds, and they are normally based in your home country, not abroad.

Chapter 10:
Public Funding

Who will fund your company when other investors want to see more development and want you to be closer to the market than you are before they invest? Could the government or the EU help fund your startup?

Public funding is an often overlooked source of financing for startups (although it isn't applicable to all startups). In this chapter you'll find out about the different types of public funding, its pros and cons and how to get it.

What is public funding?

Public funding sources are financial support programmes, targeted at startups and provided from public funds. The 'public' could be the EU, the government, municipalities or districts; even the United Nations.

But why should the public provide funding for private startup companies? Because, as we have learnt, most investors invest later in the startup process and governments believe this not only creates problems for the individual startup but also for society as a whole.

For example, say a group of university researchers have an idea for a new cure against cancer. Initially, they can start the development work in their spare-time and might even use the university lab for free, but at some point they'll need to go full-time on the project, rent their own facilities, and start to test their drugs on animals – and at that point they need funding. Just the initial phases alone can easily cost €1-5 million.

From the potential private investor's perspective, the above investment is very risky. Everyone who knows about pharmaceutical drug development knows that the chance of success (getting on the market) for such a project is smaller than one per cent, and that even if successful the company will need much more money over the next five to 10 years. In many cases, up to €1 billion is needed to bring a product to market. The individual investor, who might get 20

 © 2017 Nicolaj Højer Nielsen

per cent of the equity for investing €1 million initially, might end up with below one per cent ownership of the final company due to dilution from new investors, and with a less than one per cent chance of success. From the individual investor's point of view, such an investment won't make financial sense. Many projects find it difficult to attract private funding for these early stages of development, and despite its potentially world-changing product, won't get off the ground.

The Valley of Death for startups

The period from when the startup is initially created until it generates sufficient cash flow from revenue that it doesn't need further investors, is often referred to as the 'Valley of Death' for startups.

Initially, the cost of starting the company is often relatively low. Maybe it's only one or two developers sitting in the basement working. This can be financed via your own funds (bootstrapping) or via some of the classic early-stage investors – typically your friends, family or maybe business angels. But the cost of starting up often gets more expensive as you go along. For many IT companies, costs are associated with huge sales and marketing costs (with limited initial revenue), whereas in the previously mentioned biotech example there are huge costs of progressing with research, development and clinical trials – many years before any revenue is in sight.

This makes the hole in the ground the investment needed to keep the company running deeper and deeper, making it harder to attract early-stage investors.

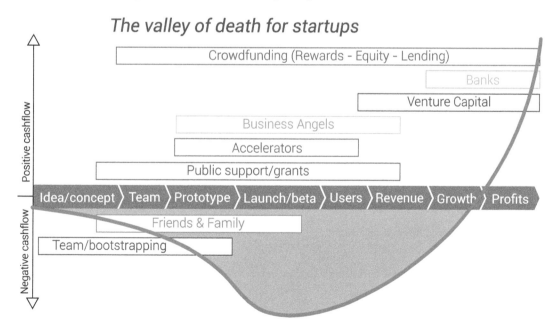

The valley of death for startups

But the 'public' sees it differently. Even a failed startup project might generate value for society that is not captured by the equity/investors alone. This can be in the form of innovation and knowledge that is spilled over to the rest of the society, but also in the creation of high-tech jobs that most governments strive to create. These are the *externalities*, meaning that an early-stage startup which is yet not attractive enough to private investors can still be of value for society in general. By providing public funding for such early-stage startup projects, the public aims to increase the creation of such companies.

Case study: Germany – public investment into High-Tech Gruenderfonds

German politicians created a public investment fund called High-Tech Gruenderfonds in partnership with a number of high-profile corporate investors, among them many of Germany's largest companies. The fund was set up to provide equity funding for high-potential technology startups in the form of seed funding of up to €500,000 per company, and with the possibility of providing of up to €2 million in follow-up financing.

This is a classic example of how European politicians have identified a funding gap (compared to Silicon Valley, for example) and attempted to close it with funds like the Gruenderfonds.

In November 2010 the advertising technology company Semasio received a €500,000 investment from High-Tech Gruenderfonds. Semasio was founded by Kasper Schou and Thomas Rask Thomsen, who had previously worked as CEO and CTO of the semantic search engine company Speed of Mind. Schou had spent the last three years working for another company in the advertising technology business, while Thomsen worked in the technology department of a bank. They wanted to create a company within behavioural targeting of online advertising, and started looking for funding.

As Kasper Schou explains:

We really didn't have much to show at that time. Not a single line of code, just a firm belief that we could make behavioural targeting work with our domain knowledge within semantic search. Behavioural targeting was an area with a very large potential but one in which companies have failed to succeed for the last decade. The issue was that the technology was quite complex to build, so we needed at least €500,000 to get started. It was therefore unlike other types of less complex software companies where you can

 © 2017 Nicolaj Højer Nielsen

build a very limited Version 1.0, start selling that to customers, and with that traction attract larger sums of funding. This was not possible in our case.

This meant five frustrating months of searching for funding where we talked with private investors, smaller venture capital funds, and even some strategic investors. But it wasn't surprising that no one would provide seed financing for a highly speculative bet on a new paradigm in behavioural profiling and targeting without the shadow of a minimum viable product.

No one except High-Tech Gruenderfonds.

I guess they believed that with our unique background and technology insights we could finally get behavioural targeting to work.

How does public funding work?

Before going into the specifics of public funding for startups, you will have to understand two basic principles: programmes change over time and most of them are local and not international.

Public funding programmes change over time

The programmes are initiated by politicians and paid for by the public. In other words, they are political projects. One government might believe it's very important to support a specific region, but the next might not. One government believes it's important to reduce CO_2 emissions, while another says it isn't or that the market can fix it.

 Key note: Expect support programmes to change!

Public funding programmes change over time and reflect the comings and goings of politicians and political agendas. Expect the available support programmes to change quickly. If you see a programme that fits your startup project, don't delay; it might be gone after the next election. And expect that some of the specific programmes mentioned in this book have already been cancelled.

Most public support programmes are created and managed by a local municipality or local government agency: they're focused on developing specific solutions for problems relating to that region. Of course, there are international programmes (most of them managed by EU-funds) but the majority are local.

The chance of a Spanish startup getting funding from a French support programme is non-existent. Of course, if that specific support programme is exceptionally attractive, you could relocate your company to that other region, but that will rarely be realistic.

 Key note: Look for funds in your home country!

What you have to look for is local public funding – specific support programmes created in the country/region/city where you're located. The support programmes mentioned in this chapter should therefore mostly be seen as inspiration for doing your own local research to find programmes relevant to your specific startup.

Types of public funding

There are hundreds of public funding programmes across Europe. Broadly speaking you can split them into three different types which together cover 99 per cent of the funds available.

Secure loans

Banks only very rarely provide loans to startups due to the high risks and the business model of banks. To offset this, governments in some countries have made it more attractive for banks to provide loans to startups by providing security for the loans. They do this in one of two ways:

1. **The startup gets the loan from the bank.** The bank is willing to provide a loan to the startup because it knows the government guarantees some of the risks. The startup still has to convince the bank that they have a viable business idea, and that the risk is not too high since the government will only provide 50 to 75 per cent security.

2. **The startup gets the loan from the governmental body.** In some countries the government has allowed the lending process to be handled partly or fully by a governmental body instead of the banks. The main reason for this is that even with the

 © 2017 Nicolaj Højer Nielsen

government guaranteeing most of the payments to banks they are reluctant to provide loans to startups. This reluctance is due to the banks' lack of experience with providing such high-risk loans since doing so doesn't fit with their traditional business model. Some governments have therefore created new government-controlled bodies that lend directly to startups.

Case Study: Penneo – loan from the Danish Growth Fund

Background: www.penneo.com is a provider of secure digital signature platforms. The company focuses on the European markets where more and more governments are issuing electronic identities (eID) to their citizens (NemID in Denmark, BankID in Norway/Sweden, for example), enabling the signing of legally binding documents online. Penneo was started in 2012 and bootstrapped the first 18 months, until the company received seed funding from a Danish venture fund and a local business angel in early 2014. By mid-2015 the company had grown rapidly in both revenue and number of users and was now cash flow positive. But should the company raise more money to grow even faster, and from which sources?

The Danish Growth Fund (Vækstfonden) is a state investment fund which invests in eq-

Penneo.com: Revenue and burn rate per month

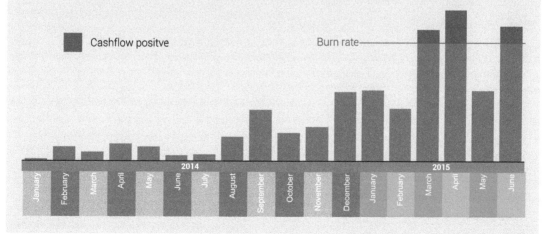

uity and provides loans and guarantees for small as well as medium-sized enterprises in collaboration with private partners and Danish financial institutions.

CEO of Penneo, Janek Borgmann explains:

Finally being early-stage positive felt so great! Now we didn't have to take in money at any cost, but could actively choose if this was right for the company, or we should grow organically instead. We had several offers from potential investors (large business angels and small VC funds) but decided this was not the right time. We still had something to prove – mainly international scalability – and this would impact the valuation of the company. We therefore decided to postpone raising a real VC round.

We didn't even consider going to a bank for a loan. Despite our huge growth, and being early-stage positive, we would still be considered too risky from the banks' perspective. Instead we approached the Danish Growth Fund and asked for one of their loans. After some meetings and providing the necessary documentation, the Danish Growth Fund provided Penneo with a loan of €275,000 at an interest rate of 10%.

From our perspective, this was a great deal. Yes, the 10% might seem high from a personal perspective, but not that bad compared to our alternatives at the time. To get the same amount of cash from an investor, we would easily have given up 10-15% of the equity in the company, and we would prefer to take it as a loan at any time.

Fast forward to the start of 2017. The money from the Danish Growth Fund enabled us to continue growing in 2015-2016, with annual growth rates of approximately 200%. Now we have also proven the international scalability of our solution, after having won our first customers in Norway, Sweden and Finland. We are now perceived as a venture capital case, and could raise an "A round" from a VC to grow even faster internationally. The question is still if that is what we really want, or if we'd rather stay in the driver's seat ourselves...

What are the downsides of a secure loan?

With the help of the government it is actually possible to get a loan from a bank for your start-up project. But there are downsides:

The paperwork. To get the loan, you will have to do the paperwork to be submitted to the bank and/or the governmental body. This work covers budgets and the business plan for the company. Depending on the body and the amount of money you're applying for, this work can be extensive and time consuming (although it isn't too different from the work and paperwork required for getting money from investors).

The liability. The main downside with government-backed loans is that the entrepreneur in many cases is personally liable for some, or all, of the amount. This goes for both loans pro-

 © 2017 Nicolaj Højer Nielsen

vided directly by the government body and those provided by banks.

Let's take an example: the startup gets the loan from the bank, but the only reason the bank is lending the money is that the bank knows that the government is providing security for 75 per cent of the loan. But before being able to go to the government for the 75 per cent, the bank has to get the money from the startup. And since the startup has limited equity (which is why they need the loan), the bank wants the entrepreneur to be personally liable. The same goes for loans provided directly via governmental bodies to startups: they want you to be personally liable for the loan.

Sometimes you can negotiate out of being personally liable for the loan – either in full or partially. Ask your bank and the public body (in charge of the loan support programmes) about their requirements with regards to this!

 Key note: Are you willing to be personally liable or not?

Is it worth the risk? It depends on the individual case (and what alternative funding is available) and also the willingness to take that kind of personal risk from the founder's perspective. Given that most startups go bankrupt, the risk of you ending up with a lot of personal debt is high.

Equity financing

One alternative to a loan is to get equity investment. Governments across the EU (and the EU itself) put public money into different investment funds to stimulate equity investments in startups. This is done by investing in existing VC funds where the governments become 'limited partners'. In fact, governments and various investment bodies from the EU are often the biggest investors in what are believed to be private VC funds.

But the public also invest directly into startups! This is done by creating independent investment funds funded by public money.

The investment criteria differ from fund to fund, and depend on the perceived need by politicians in the individual country. Some of the funds act (more or less) as VC funds, meaning they are looking for the next big thing and are willing to take high risks. Others are more focused on providing funding for specific industries or regions where they have identified a funding gap in the private market.

Denmark: Public innovation centres

In Denmark, the government is trying to fight the Valley of Death via the creation of public innovation centres that invest public money primarily as equity into startups.

The money is taken from the budget of the Ministry of Higher Education and Science, but instead of investing directly into startups, the ministry has appointed four public innovation centres (Borean, SDTI, Pre-Seed Innovation and CapNova) who do the screening and investment on their behalf.

Investments per year and by industry

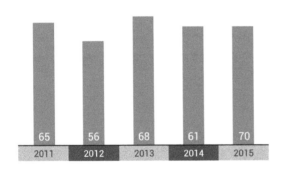

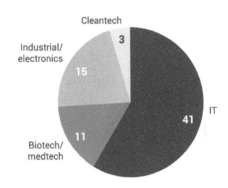

They invest in approximately 70 new companies per year (in comparison there are approximately 10 to 15 venture capital investments per year in the country), with the majority of investments happening within the IT industry, followed by the biotech/medico and industrial/electronic industries.

The industries invested in reflect that the innovation centres are looking for high risk/high reward projects. They seek something that can become 'big' like venture capital companies, but because projects are being funded with public money they are willing to invest much earlier. The initial investment is typically in the range of €400,000. In return, the Public innovation Centre typically receives a 20 to 40 per cent stake in the company (to be negotiated on an individual basis).

One example of a company receiving such investment is MotilityCount; the previously mentioned medtech company that developed a sperm-quality test for home use. At the time the company received investment from an innovation centre (2011), it was very early days. There was a simple prototype, a patent application and some preliminary data that indicated that the device might work, but there was still a lot of development work to be done and the market potential of the device was also uncertain. It was a very risky project at that time and it was unlikely that the company could have received funding from a venture capital fund. But the public innovation centre was willing to take the risk, and invested a total of €500,000 in collaboration with a local business angel.

 © 2017 Nicolaj Højer Nielsen

The downside of (public) equity financing

As with any financing there are downsides to having the public as a co-investor in your start-up.

Loss of ownership. These public investment bodies have to invest on 'market terms', both in order to avoid lawsuits relating to the subsidising of private companies with public funds, and to avoid outcompeting the same private investors which the public try to build an ecosystem around. This means 20 to 40 per cent ownership in a classic venture capital style deal. Whether it's worth it must be decided on a case-by-case basis. If your alternative is being unable to create the company due to a lack of private investors, it might be OK to have 60 to 80 per cent left after the fund has had its share.

Lack of control. Public funds not only try to mimic private funds in terms of equity but also in terms of protecting provisions when investing. They might only own 20 per cent of your company but they still have negotiating terms where they control the board and have veto rights, so in reality they are in control of the company.

Smart money? Whether the lack of control is worth the money also depends on who is then in control. Unlike private VC funds (and business angels), the majority of 'managers' at public investment funds have limited entrepreneurial experience themselves and have spent the majority of their career in large private or public organisations. You should therefore ask yourself whether you want to have a fund bureaucrat sitting on your board. What is the quality of the advice you will receive from them? This is of course very much dependent on the specific fund and the manager of that fund.

 Key note: Is the governmental fund providing you with smart money?

You should do your own due diligence on the fund and its manager before accepting an investment from them – just like with any other private investor. Do you think they can provide value to your company? And if not, would you still accept the money, or is the risk of your company being taken over by a public servant with no entrepreneurial experience so high you'd rather decline the offer?

© 2017 Nicolaj Højer Nielsen

Grants and co-financing

There is a third form of public funding in the form of public grants. This is attractive in that you won't have to repay the grant or give equity in return. Why should governments give money to startups without getting anything in return?

Governments provide grants based on the assumption there is a market failure with funding for a specific activity and there are externalities, so it's good for the government to make grants available even though it's at a cost. They do get something back.

The difference is that they believe these activities wouldn't have happened without the grant. In other words, the key for success to getting public grants comes down to two things:

1. The business idea helps the government achieve their goal
2. The government is convinced you couldn't have continued otherwise

The first point is that governments do *not* give money out to *all* startups, but only to those that can help the government meet a specific societal or socio-economic goal. In order to get a grant, the startup needs to know what they can help the government achieve. They need to find out what kind of support programmes have been created to achieve specific government goals (for example, improving jobs in certain industries, getting university research grants or advancing clean environment projects).

Then comes the very important second point which many startups miss when applying for public grants: the government only gives grants to startups when they believe the startup would not be able to continue otherwise! If that isn't the case, the money could have been better spent elsewhere, since the goal of the government is *not* to support your company but to achieve its own goals (by having more startups working on them).

In other words, you will have to convince the funding body not only that your startup can help them achieve their goals but also that you cannot proceed without the grant!

Points to keep in mind when applying for public grants

So how do you ensure your startup gets the public grant out of the many that apply? You can improve your chances by having the following points in mind:

1. If you're not a grant application expert, hire one!

To be fair to everyone, the government requires you to fill out plenty of paperwork to apply for grants. You need to include information about what you want to achieve and how you can help them achieve their goals.

 © 2017 Nicolaj Højer Nielsen

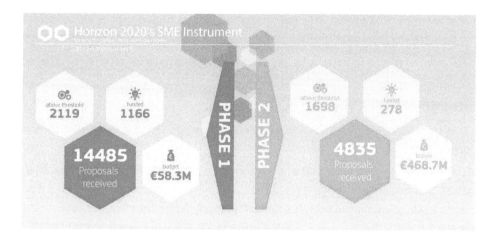

There is of course huge competition for such public grants. The infographic below shows statistics for one of the largest public grants in Europe, the Horizon 2020 SME Instruments managed by the EU, where Phase 1 is the small grants (up to €50,000) and Phase 2 (the large grants of up to €2.5 million). For Phase 1 applications, eight per cent got funding and for Phase 2, fewer than six per cent were successful.

They base their decision on the paperwork you submit. This is unlike approaching a VC fund or business angel where the personal relationship is key and you need an introduction. Wining and dining matters much less to get this type of funding; what you write down matters much more. You can get a conventional venture capitalist to invest in your startup if you're a fantastic person with charisma and a strong network and you've done it all before. But that's no use if you apply for a public grant and write a poor application. You won't get the grant even if your idea is great and you have a strong team to back it.

 Key note: Don't send in your application if it isn't perfect

If you don't have the time (typically at least a hundred hours) to produce a brilliant application, don't send it in because there will be so much competition you won't get the grant.

It is not only about the time you put in, but also the skill and experience involved in communicating what you've done. It's difficult to convince (in writing) a public body that your project may help achieve a public-interest goal and at the same time make a case for why you won't be able to complete the project without a grant. That's why experience in writing applications is key. Either you have the skills and the time or you use a grant consultant who has that experience. These consultants have success rates much higher than average, and the difference lies in knowing exactly what the specific public fund is looking for and how to communicate this. Despite the fee consultants charge, startups are often better off hiring them.

• •

 ### Key note: Check the consultant's skills!

Do your own due diligence on the grant consultant if you're considering hiring one. Ask about them in your network and talk to some of their former clients if possible. Also try to negotiate a fee structure that not only includes a fixed fee for writing the application, but also a success fee in case the application goes through so you maximise the chances of the consultant doing a good job.

• •

2. You need co-financing!

The time it takes to produce a good quality application, and the bureaucracy involved in evaluating the application, means it normally takes at least three to six months from application to grant. On top of this, most grants are paid as cost-reimbursement. The grant is paid *after* the cost has been incurred, leading to further need for short-term liquidity even if you get the grant. But you also need co-financing for the grant itself. Normally the grants don't cover a hundred per cent of the cost. For most public grants, the percentage of cost covered by the grant is between 50 and 75 per cent.

In the above-mentioned example, EU SME Instruments, the grant covers up to 70 per cent of the total cost. The startup must then fund the remaining 30 per cent or find other external funding.

But if the public really want to achieve its goals, why don't they pay a hundred per cent of the costs? Saving money is one reason, but another is that they want to ensure incentive on behalf of the entrepreneur.

Imagine if they paid a hundred per cent of the costs for a project. This would lead to a ton of applications from startups just to get their salaries paid. These would most likely be projects with a lower chance of success since the startups' motivations are flawed.

The government is looking to strike a balance with its grants: they want to invest in things that help the public achieve its goals and where there is incentive for doing so, but this can't be done if the entrepreneur must cover a hundred per cent of the costs.

Even with a government grant you need co-financing. It is however much easier to attract private investors (for example business angels) if you can go to them and say 75 per cent of the cost is already covered with a public grant!

 © 2017 Nicolaj Højer Nielsen

! Key note: Prove co-financing

An important part of the grant application process is to show in a credible way that you can get that co-investment. Imagine being a small startup and asking for a €5 million grant where you might need €2 million in co-financing. You don't need to have the co-financing secured before you apply, but you need to convince the grant giver that it will be possible for you to secure this co-financing. This can include letters of intent from current investors saying they have more money to put in if you get the grant, or from potential investors (e.g. VCs, angels) who will document their interest in the project. This will show credibility and improve your chance of a positive review of your application.

Case study: Sepior receives €2 million from EU

Sepior is a Danish cyber security company that was founded in 2013 when it received €500,000 in funding from both a local seed fund and business angels.

In 2015 the initial product (encryption software to protect cloud data from hacking) was finalised and tested by a number of potential customers. Sepior, together with some partners, applied for EU funding of approximately €2,300,000 to be used for further R&D and further market development. The money was provided by the EU support programme SME Instruments Phase 2, which provides public grants up to €2,500,000 to cover up to 70 per cent of project costs.

Why was Sepior (of which the author of this book is co-founder) successful in their grant application?

1. Sepior found a public grant topic that fitted them very well. The specific SME instrument topic was:

The Open and Disruptive Innovation (ODI) scheme aims to foster the development of fast-growing, innovative SMEs with promising, close-to market ideas bearing high disruptive potential in terms of products, services, models, and markets.

Here was a grant allocation clearly aimed at SMEs like Sepior, who were close to market (the core product was already developed) and had disruptive potential. Sepior had developed a ground-breaking technology that had the potential to disrupt the way we protect cloud data; all in all, a very good fit between grant topic and the project.

2. Sepior had a very strong team with external support:

Sepior is lucky to have a world-class technical team and one of its co-founders is one of the most cited researchers in the world within cryptography. This was a very important part of the successful grant application. In addition, Sepior asked outside opinion leaders in IT security to write letters of support which they included in the application. These letters gave even more credibility to the team.

3. Sepior showed credible co-financing:

When a relatively small startup asks for a €2 million grant, that pays up to 70 per cent of the costs, you don't need a maths degree to figure out they also need significant co-financing.

To improve the credibility of our application, and in order to convince the grant body we could secure such co-financing, we asked both existing and potential investors to demonstrate their interest in co-financing via letters of intent we included in the application. Together with extensive calculations on how we would cover the financing needs, that documentation was essential for us getting a positive review of our application.

4. Sepior spent a lot of time and used external experts:

The team behind Sepior was lucky that some of them had extensive experience in writing other EU grant applications while others had extensive experience in writing business plans and investor material. Compared to the average startup, we had the skills needed to write the application, and we literally spent hundreds of hours on it.

The first time we submitted the application it didn't get over the threshold. This highlights both the tough competition and how hard it is to write an application if you haven't applied for the specific grant before and don't know exactly what the evaluators are looking for.

After the first attempt, we were close to the goal and decided to ask an outside expert to review our application and propose changes. The input from that expert, and the further hundreds of hours spent on revising the application, were essential for getting the grant the second time we applied.

 © 2017 Nicolaj Højer Nielsen

Take-away points

Public funding is financial support by the public at a local, regional, national or EU-level.

They provide funding because they believe there is a gap between where a startup hits huge costs and where a private investor will want to invest, and also because addressing this market failure is of public interest and has public value potential.

Public funding is offered in the form of loans, equity and grants. To get these funds you need to realise the government is offering financing to help you achieve your goals, and you have to understand how your startup can help the government achieve their goals.

You need to look for specific support programmes that fit your profile. Competition is fierce for many of the public support programmes, so only the best applications get selected. You will need to invest considerable time and probably get expert help in making your application to successfully secure public funding.

Chapter 11:
Banks

Many entrepreneurs believe a good place to go when looking for funding for their startup project is their bank. This is probably because it's familiar and perceived as more accessible, and besides banks lend money and money is what startups need, right? Case closed.

Not quite. At the end of this chapter you will understand why this is not so and why banks turn down the vast majority of entrepreneurs who request funding for their startup project.

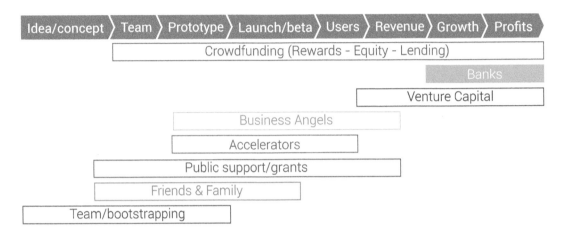

How do banks provide financing?

Let's think like a banker. A financier provides capital or funding for an entity in one of two ways: equity or loans. The key difference is in the business model:

1. **Equity:** the financier takes a share in your company and hopes you will be profitable or get sold.

2. **Loans:** the financer makes a loan and hopes the company will be able to pay the loan back with interest.

In the case of equity, the financier gives a company €1 million in return for, say, a 20 per cent stake in the company. That is equity: the financier owns shares in the company. The money they provide will not be paid back, but they will get dividends if the company becomes profitable or capital gains if it's sold. This is how business angels and venture capital funds work.

In the case of loans, the financier lends money to be paid back. They won't own shares in the company, but will be repaid with interest. This is how banks work. Banks provide access to credit in the form of loans. That's their business model.

If a company goes bankrupt, the bank sometimes ends up with shares in the company as part of the liquidation process. However, banks don't want to own companies – unless they are forced to.

 © 2017 Nicolaj Højer Nielsen

Risk versus reward for equity versus debt

Providing debt instead of equity has a huge impact on the risk and reward for a bank.

If the business becomes very successful, the debt holders won't get a share of that upside. The banks will just get the loan repaid with interest.

For example, the entrepreneur Morten Lund was friends with the guys who created Skype, and when they started out they didn't have any money. Lund let them use his apartment as office space and helped them get started. He got a few shares in Skype in return. Those few shares ended up being worth more than €10 million. Imagine if he had offered the founders of Skype a loan instead of taking equity!

On the risk side of things, the bank should in theory have less risk than shareholders. When you own shares in the company, you only get your money after debt holders (the bank) have got theirs. Let's assume I'm a financier who owns 20 per cent of a company that has €5 million in cash but owes €4 million to a bank. I can't just take 20 percent of the €5 million. The €4 million goes to the bank first and then the equity holders share the remaining €1 million, according to priority and the size of their holdings. So the equity holders only get money if the debt holders have been paid back. The debt holders are always first in line.

Banks have therefore less downside than equity holders because if something goes wrong, they get their money first. However, they also get less of an upside.

 Key note to entrepreneurs: Banks don't care about your 'billion-dollar opportunity'

Banks don't care how big your company may become, however a business angel, who is in on the upside since he owns shares in the company, will be excited at your prospects. On the other hand, your bank will probably be scared and think your idea sounds very risky.

What does all this mean for startups?

For startups there is very rarely money left for debt holders when they go bankrupt. Most startups have very limited assets that can be sold afterwards, since they often spend the money on either R&D or sales and marketing, where the 'scrap value' of such assets is close to zero when doing a fire-sale after a bankruptcy.

In other words, the banks have almost the same level of risk as investors/shareholders, but with no upside if a startup like Skype gets sold for billions.

It's therefore no surprise that banks don't usually lend out money to startups. However, many first-time entrepreneurs make the mistake of thinking banks want to invest in small and risky businesses and see them grow into large and successful businesses. They don't! Banks only say yes to companies in the low risk quadrants.

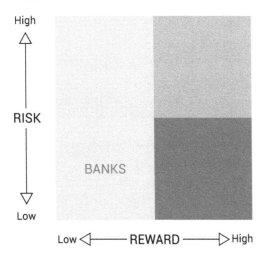

As a new startup that has not proven itself, you are never a low risk case. Statistics show that early-stage startups are inherently high risk. You might become lower risk over time when you have proved the business works, but early-stage startups are never low risk.

Why not try other banks?

If a bank has refused to give a startup a loan, the entrepreneur will often speak to other banks. The idea is to shop around for a 'better' bank. In most cases this won't work. The first bank entrepreneurs typically go to is their current bank where the entrepreneur may have personal contacts and where there is a remote chance of a loan. If and when you go to another bank, where you and your credit history aren't known, the chance of a loan is even lower. This is because banks value their relationships and history with their clients since this reduces the perceived risk. If you walk in the door of a bank that doesn't know you and ask for a loan for a startup, this will almost certainly not end with a loan.

· ·

 Key note: Your existing bank is almost always your best bet

Don't believe shopping around and talking with new banks will solve your startup's liquidity issues. Since they don't know you, they will be even more reluctant to offer you a loan. Your existing bank is therefore your best bet.

· ·

 © 2017 Nicolaj Højer Nielsen

When do banks provide loans for startups?

Of course, there are instances where you can get a startup loan from a bank:

The bank will give your startup money:

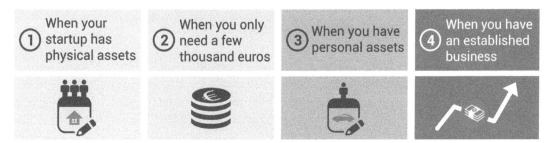

| 1 When your startup has physical assets | 2 When you only need a few thousand euros | 3 When you have personal assets | 4 When you have an established business |

Or even better, a combination of the above.

1. Startups with physical assets

There are, of course, startups with physical assets. Banks will still consider them high risk, but they may have assets that will satisfy a bank because these assets make a risk evaluation feasible. If you have a machine, a car, property or land they believe they can resell if you go bankrupt, the bank may feel more confident in making an evaluation. Banks think like this: if you spend the loan on five cars, they can sell them for 50 per cent of the market price even if you go bankrupt.

You still face an uphill struggle because you have to convince the bank that your startup, with no proof of revenue, has assets the bank can sell if you go bankrupt. They still won't try to understand your business, but they'll just be a little less concerned because you have physical assets.

2. You only want a few thousand euros

If you're looking for a small sum to start your business, build a prototype, or to start your consulting company, and you don't have any paying customers for the next six months, you can probably get a loan for a few thousand euros. With most banks, if you have a good credit history and have been a good customer, they will provide you with some kind of credit line. Whether that is two or ten thousand euros depends on who you are and what your credit history looks like.

Of course, you'll be personally liable for the loan; banks won't lend the money to the company. The bank will basically say, 'You're young, you have a degree, and you could get a *real* job, so you'll be able to pay it back even if your company goes bankrupt.'

3. You have personal assets

On the other hand, if you actually have assets (a house or a car with no debts) then you can put those assets up as collateral against a loan. Again, the banks won't lend money to the company, but they lend the money to you because they know that since you have these assets, you'll be able to repay it.

4. You have an established business

The bank-funded business model is best for when you own an established business and have shown you have customers who are paying your invoices. In that case, you can go to your bank and get a credit line because that's what banks like. They like existing businesses that need liquidity.

If you produce a product in the first month, you deliver in the third, and the customers pay in the sixth, you need liquidity. If you have been in business for one or two years and the banks can see your customers like the product, then you can get a credit line for liquidity.

This also involves factoring, where you sell your accounts receivable to a lender who then gives you the money now (with a discount) so you don't have to wait the (say) three to six months until the customer pays its bills. The lender can be a bank or another entity specialised in factoring.

Take-away points

Banks operate a low risk, low return strategy. It makes perfect sense for banks not to lend money to startups, even at high interest rates, because they can't evaluate the risk and aren't in on the upside. Banks are therefore rarely the first source or major source of capital for startups.

You must realise that banks won't lend you money for developing your idea into a business. Only go to a bank for funding if you only want a few thousand euros for liquidity, you have personal assets you are prepared to forfeit, your business has assets, you have an established business with a stable history, or robust accounts payable that you can use for factoring.

 © 2017 Nicolaj Højer Nielsen

© 2017 Nicolaj Højer Nielsen

Chapter 12

Crowdfunding

One of the most hyped areas of startup funding is crowdfunding. The various forms of crowdfunding provide new ways to fund your startup, from the earliest days until very late in the development of the company. But it's much harder – and more expensive – than most startups think to run a successful crowdfunding campaign.

This chapter introduces you to crowdfunding for startups, and helps you consider which type of crowdfunding (if any) is suitable for your startup. You'll also learn when such a funding method is beneficial for your company and when it has the best chance of success.

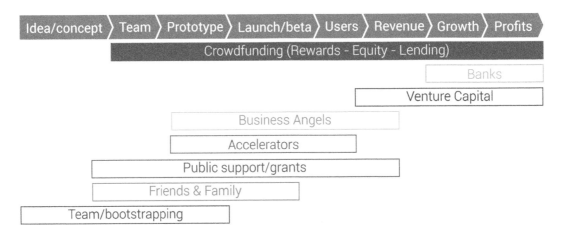

What is crowdfunding?

Crowdfunding is a very broad term used to describe projects, companies or causes that are financed by many small 'donors' instead of a few large ones. One of the most successful and famous examples is when Barack Obama used crowdfunding to raise $750 million for his 2008 presidential election campaign. Of that figure, almost 50% consisted of donations of less than $200.

Crowdfunding is carried out online, mostly using a platform such as Kickstarter or Crowd-Cube which acts as an intermediary between the funder and the entrepreneur. The platform receives a percentage of the funding in return for hosting and marketing the campaign to the platform's current user base.

Types of crowdfunding relevant for startups

Because of its different forms and many different applications, crowdfunding causes a lot of confusion among founders. Of the four main types of crowdfunding, only three are relevant for startups.

 © 2017 Nicolaj Højer Nielsen

What are the different crowdfunding models?

Source: Colins et al. (2013)

The donation-based model of crowdfunding is a means to raise funding for charities or social and/or charitable projects, and is therefore not that relevant to for-profit ventures. This leaves three other types of crowdfunding which are of interest to startup companies:

Type	Description
Reward	In reward-based crowdfunding, the 'crowd' pays you up front for a service/product you intend to provide. In return the 'backers' typically receive either the product (when it has been made) or a small token of gratitude (e.g. a handwritten postcard). For larger donations, additional rewards are devised. Typical donation/payment is €10–€100 per backer per project, and the amounts raised vary significantly from project to project. Most successful reward-based crowdfunding campaigns raise €5,000–€50,000 from hundreds of backers.
Equity	In this crowdfunding model, the 'backers' are buying shares in your company instead of the product itself (even though many companies promise free products to their shareholders). The size of the funding goal varies between platform types (and sometimes between projects on the same platform). But most successful equity crowdfunding campaigns are in the range of €50,000–€500,000 from hundreds of different investors.
Lending	In crowdlending, the crowd lends money to the company and receives interest on the borrowed amount. In other words, it acts as a bank at a stage when banks won't offer a loan. The amount raised via crowdlending varies from company to company but often the company borrows €50,000–€500,000, with the amount typically spread among hundreds of different lenders.

Which companies do crowdfunders back?

In crowdfunding, individual backers tend to display the following three characteristics, meaning that their 'investment decisions' are based on different criteria from those of other types of investor:

1 **They are private individuals:** Most crowdfunders are private individuals and not professional investors. This has a huge impact on the kinds of project they will support. Whereas professional investors like business angels and venture capitalists (VCs) focus on the risk/reward of the project, this often doesn't carry the same weight for crowdfunders. They invest for other reasons, often because they feel a connection to the project or company they want to support.

2 **They often don't know you:** Crowdfunders don't need to know who you are. As most crowdfunding campaigns are funded by hundreds of different backers, your close friends normally make up only a small fraction of those. Unlike friends who invest because they know and trust you, and VCs/angels who spend a lot of time getting to know you, most of the crowdfunders have never heard of you or only knew of you via friends of friends before they saw your project in a crowdfunding campaign.

3 **They invest quickly:** As crowdfunders typically invest much smaller amounts, they tend to spend very little time evaluating whether they want to back/invest in/lend to a given company. Often, they spend only a few minutes evaluating the uploaded content before they decide. This is very different from other funding sources, where the large amounts at stake mean that the investors spend weeks or even months evaluating your case.

Although most crowdfunders are motivated by many other reasons than financial outcomes, you can still categorise their preferred types of project according to the risk/reward matrix:

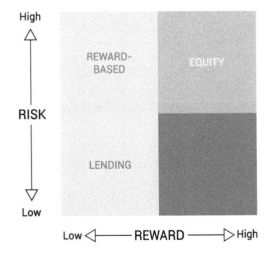

© 2017 Nicolaj Højer Nielsen

Reward-based crowdfunding – High risk/low reward

Backing a reward-based crowdfunding campaign doesn't strictly make sense from a risk/ reward perspective. Crowdfunders receive a discount (compared to future retail price) and maybe even a handwritten thank you card, but this is a minimal reward in comparison to owning shares in a successful startup. There is also a risk inherent in paying up front for a yet-to-be-developed product that might not be as good as expected and may be delayed. You should wait until the product has been successfully developed and tested before buying if you want to minimise the risk of being disappointed. But their reasons for backing a project are often not rational; instead they feel a connection to the product being developed and/or the people behind the project. This means that they are willing to back even high risk/low reward projects.

Equity crowdfunding – High risk/high reward

In theory, equity could be crowdfunded from all the other three quadrants of the matrix. In reality, it is mainly high risk/high reward projects that are crowdfunded this way. This is mostly owing to the fact that the crowdfunders are private individuals who don't invest solely for financial gain, but also owing to the excitement of being a shareholder in something fun that could potentially be 'the next big thing'. In addition, a significant part of these equity crowdfunders are actually friends & family investors who use the equity crowdfunding platform to structure their investment in the startup (meaning that the investors are people you know already, who just use the platform to ease the administrative work in doing the investor round).

Crowdlending – Low risk/low reward

Crowdlending is different in that funders neither receive the product (as in reward crowdfunding) nor are part of the financial upside (as in equity crowdfunding). Each of the crowdfunders is acting as a one-person bank, lending out small amounts to the startup. With no upside, they are of course looking for *relatively* low risk/low reward opportunities. This means that the risk/reward for the backer is low compared to other types of startup investment.

At what stage does crowdfunding work?

Crowdfunding can be a lifeline for startups because it bridges the early stage funding gap of the company, when the project is considered too risky for professional investors and banks. Because of the investor profile and the smaller investments per backer (lower risk), many startups now turn to crowdfunding at a stage when other investor types would not be prepared to invest.

However, because of the differences between the different crowdfunding types, each is more likely to be successful at a different stage in your startup. This is illustrated below.

Reward-based

Reward-based crowdfunding is possible from the very early days of the startup. The limiting factor is that you need something to show your 'backers', to get them excited about your new product, as they are very unlikely to support you based on just an idea. Typically, successfully crowdfunded companies have a strong team (demonstrated industry expertise) and at least a semi-functional prototype to show. Some platforms (owing to some frauds in previous campaigns) now even require startups to showcase real pictures of their products/prototypes instead of computer-animated visualisations, thereby reducing the risk to backers by forcing startups to wait until it's more likely they can successfully develop the intended product before starting their campaign.

Equity

To be successful, it's normally more realistic to start equity crowdfunding later in the process than a reward-based campaign. Most of the startups that fund via these channels have developed their first product and in many cases have both users/customers and revenue to show. The reason for this is that the backers' motivation for funding is not only the love of the product, but also the hope of making a good financial investment. They also tend to 'invest' a bit more money compared to reward-based backers (€1,000 vs €50) and therefore expect to see more proof as they are taking a higher personal risk.

Lending

Crowdlenders fund even later in the process, typically only after the company has shown significant revenue or even when the company has managed to remain 'cash-flow positive' (spending less money than is coming in from revenue) for months or years. This 'traction' is needed because the money is provided as a loan, similar to one from a bank, so the funders have no financial upside besides interest. To offset the missing upside they want a low risk of bankruptcy and to know that the company has managed to develop and sell the product. However, whereas banks will normally offer a loan only after the company has shown profits for several years, private crowdlenders tend to go in earlier and are okay with a shorter track record. As an example, the platform Funding Circle requires that companies who want to crowdlend via their platform have 2+ years of filed accounts and an annual turnover of at least £50,000.

In the following sections we'll go into detail about the opportunities and risks inherent in each type of crowdfunding.

Reward-based crowdfunding

It is possible to set up a reward-based crowdfunding campaign on your own website and to ask potential backers to pay you money up front in return for a product you intend to make. In reality this is very hard to administer (in terms of development, marketing, managing payments, etc.). Most startups therefore do the crowdfunding campaign on an established platform, either one with a presence in their own country or one of the two global players – Kickstarter and Indiegogo.

	KICKSTARTER https://www.kickstarter.com/	INDIEGOGO https://www.indiegogo.com/
DESCRIPTION	The biggest crowdfunding site, with 12 million backers having pledged almost $3 billion to 121,000 successfully funded projects.	A smaller platform covering more countries, with 2.5 million backers having pledged more than $800 million to more than 175,000 different projects.
FEE STRUCTURE	Charges 5% of money raised + 3% in credit card fees.	Charges 5% of money raised + 3% in credit card fees.
FUNDING	Fixed (all or nothing: only if the campaign reaches its funding target).	Fixed (all or nothing) or flexible (the project receives whatever is raised).
SUCCESS RATES	36% meet the funding target, with $103.3 million raised for the top 500 campaigns in 2016.	17% meet the funding target (although flexible funding campaigns are paid if the target isn't met), with $71.7 million raised for the top 500 campaigns in 2016.
AVAILABLE IN	17 countries, most prominently in the US.	Over 200 countries.
PROS	The most well-known Kickstarter projects get more coverage and more of a 'buzz', and the fact that there are fewer 'live' campaigns (and therefore less competition) means that projects have a better chance to become a 'featured campaign'.	Campaigns are automatically accepted and a working prototype isn't necessary to start a campaign. It's also possible to continue funding after the campaign period ends. Pledges, however, are non-refundable, meaning that there's no drop-off.
CONS	A working product prototype is required – and funding can be withdrawn after fundraising if this doesn't happen. The platform does not accept startups that develop medical products.	There are fewer backers and so less coverage. Campaigns are not driven by the urgency of all-or-nothing funding, so targets are met less often.

When a startup pitches its idea on a crowdfunding platform, it asks for a predefined amount of funding in return for different non-financial rewards. The size of the reward depends on the size of the contribution a backer makes, and it may take the form of the product, gifts or other non-financial benefits. Based on the pitch, the crowd decides whether to support the project or not.

If the target amount is reached within a given time period (usually 30–60 days) the creator receives the money and promises to deliver the rewards to his backers. Campaigns on most crowdfunding platforms are all or nothing, i.e. if the target amount is not reached within the time period, supporters are not charged and the initiator does not receive any funds.

There are a number of differences between the fee structures on different platforms, and each works slightly differently, but the basic value proposition to the startups remains more or less the same. The platform helps you organise reward-based crowdfunding campaigns in return for a commission.

Benefits of reward-based crowdfunding

There are two main potential benefits to be gained by funding a startup via a reward-based campaign:

Liquidity (avoid other investors): From a liquidity perspective, a successful reward-based crowdfunding campaign is ideal. You get the money up front for a product you are in the process of making but might not deliver to your customers for another 6–18 months. That money makes a significant difference to an early-stage startup. You may 'only' raise €50,000, but compare this to raising the same amount from friends or business angels, where you would quickly have to give at least 10% of the equity in return. Even if you are happy to do this, it can be hard to raise the initial money at such an early stage. With reward-based crowdfunding you must only give your product in return, and you get the money up front.

Market validation (attract other investors/partners): For most startups the market validation provided by a reward-based campaign is of even higher importance. For all early-stage start-ups, 'Is there really a need for this product?' is the biggest question in investors' minds. What better way to prove this than to show that people are willing to pay up front for a product you have yet to develop? This will impress all investors, and successful crowdfunding campaigns will help a lot in your future fundraising efforts. But this market validation isn't only good for use with investors – you can use it with other partners you want to impress, too. Many crowdfunding campaigns are in fact partly or wholly marketing stunts, with the major aim not of selling a lot of products to end-customers but, rather, using the attention/PR from the campaign to generate interest from partners and distributors.

 © 2017 Nicolaj Højer Nielsen

Case study: LABFRESH – Get your product in the hands of real people

LABFRESH produces odour-, stain- and wrinkle-proof dress shirts for men. The company ran two successful crowdfunding campaigns to launch its product in early 2017. Founder Kasper Brandi Petersen tells how his marketing focused on the product's appeal:

'No fashion companies were interested in stain- and smell-repellent clothing because it was very expensive to produce and it would make their customers buy less clothes due to improved product lifetime. Luckily I just spent three years building an aspirational fashion service, so I thought why not try to bring this technology to market?

'Reward-based crowdfunding was for us entirely about finding product–market fit. When I launch a new startup I want to be able to work on it for 5+ years so I needed to know if this technology had enough potential to make it worth my time. As it was, we raised €30,000 on Indiegogo and €151,000 on Kickstarter. When the campaign ran, we were the number one fashion project on both platforms, which also tells you something about the scope of the two platforms: Kickstarter has a much broader reach than Indiegogo.

'We knew the minimum target needed to be reachable within the first 38 hours of our campaign – if you achieve that, you can get a lot of media attention and Kickstarter might select you as a "project we love", as they did with us. That gives you incredible traction for no marketing spend.

'The value of our product is very easy to communicate – by showing a picture of red wine hitting a white shirt and 1–2 lines of text, we can clearly show what we are all about. If your product is too complicated or narrow, you will have a hard time raising money on crowdfunding platforms. In total we spent €14,000 on ads via our agency and my homemade creations for the Dutch and Danish markets. This is lower than many other campaigns with similar funding results.

'We only had 122 email signups and 330 Facebook followers when we launched. Instead, we focused on prepping journalists and influencers so they would test our shirts and post stellar reviews in the first 24 hours. Your network can provide revenue the first couple of days, but it does not scale the same way as influencer and media mentions. The media attention activated our network because it made them proud to share these stories about someone they knew. We also organised a Thunderclap so 160 people would post on Facebook at the same time when we went live. My advice is to get your product in the hands of real people; they need to see and feel the magic.

'We were supposed to close a smaller angel round via our network next month but we have now been convinced that equity crowdfunding gives us a lot of benefits besides the money – mainly one more group of excited ambassadors. So instead of an angel round, we will now do a convertible debt note via a Dutch platform called Symbid, at very attractive terms due to the customer validation we received via the successful Kickstarter campaign.'

Cons of reward-based crowdsourcing – from a funding perspective

Despite its potential, there are also possible downsides to running a reward-based crowd-funding campaign:

1. **Not reaching the goal:** Most crowdfunding campaigns don't reach the goals set by the founders; for instance, in 2016, just 36% of Kickstarter campaigns and 17% on Indiegogo reached their funding goals. This can have severe consequences for startups. On the majority of platforms, campaigns are run on an 'all-or-nothing' basis, meaning that if they don't meet their goals, they receive no funding at all. Even when they do receive what was pledged, it may be less than they need to develop their product, making it hard to deliver to backers by the promised date. Worse, this is a very public way to fail. Not reaching your funding goals can have a negative impact on the start-up's image, which can affect your ability to raise further money elsewhere.

   Also, it's the lowest funding goals that have the highest success rates. Because most platforms take an 'all-or-nothing' approach, the chances of having a successful campaign decrease as the target value goes up. Kickstarter, the world's most popular reward-based crowdfunding platform, reports that 38% of campaigns with a $10,000 funding target are successful, compared to just 18% when the goal is $50,000.

- -

 Key note: Set a low funding goal

Setting your funding goals on a crowdfunding platform requires careful consideration. You know the minimum you need to continue, but set your goal too high and you may lose it all. Setting a low goal is a smart move, because it means getting your money and being perceived as a success. This boosts confidence in other investors, making it easier to secure funding elsewhere.

 © 2017 Nicolaj Højer Nielsen

Remember, a low goal is not a limit! Clever campaigns set 'stretch goals' beyond their original targets to keep investors motivated after the main funding goal has been reached.

- -

(2) You need further funding BECAUSE of the crowdfunding campaign: An unexpected but common side-effect of a successful crowdfunding campaign is the need to raise more money! In general, startups underestimate the money they need to finalise their product, especially when it comes to putting physical products into production.

Running a crowdfunding campaign suddenly results in promising your product to a lot of customers, often at a very low/attractive price. Although you have money from the campaign, the campaign itself will often force you to quickly go back into fundraising mode to cover the costs related to fulfilling your promises.

(3) You can't deliver on your promises (leading to 'death by Kickstarter' and/or limited flexibility): What's worse than a failed crowdfunding campaign? A successful crowdfunding campaign where you can't deliver on your promises. Often, because the product is much harder and/or more expensive to make than expected, this leads to delayed delivery or inability to deliver at all. Instead of your backers becoming future ambassadors for your product, they complain very loudly indeed! This risk by itself has another potential downside: that the startup loses its flexibility owing to the campaign. While it may discover that it makes sense to abandon the product or significantly change its specifications, the startup will try to avoid this at almost any cost to avoid damaging its reputation. The initial enthusiasm and publicity for the product can backfire.

Case study: Airtame– Unhappy backers must be appeased

Airtame ran Europe's then highest-ever funded crowdfunding campaign in 2014, raising $1.3million for its HDMI dongle. After crowdfunding, the startup found itself under immense pressure to fulfil 15,000 orders in half the necessary time and half the budget. Shortcuts had to be made and the product was eventually released with less functionality than backers were promised.

Funders were understandably angry and the company had to deal with hundreds of emails as well as angry complaints on social media. Co-founder and CEO Jonas Gyalokay explains how Airtame won back the confidence of its backers:

'We decided that the only way to do this properly would be to go the extra mile for the customers. Every. Single. Time. Because of its initial shortcomings, our product needed all the support that we could give it.

Source: indiegogo.com

'Hundreds of hours and thousands of emails later, we are now receiving daily appreciation for our support. We build relations and create ambassadors. The results are tangible. Have a look at our Trustpilot and Amazon reviews. A lot of people mention our customer service.'

The company's approach worked – Airtame raised further seed capital of $1.4 million and expanded its team to over 30 people in Denmark and the US by July 2016.

It takes a lot of effort! Probably the biggest disadvantage of reward-based crowdsourcing as a funding channel is the effort it takes to make a successful crowdfunding campaign. In theory, you could just upload your pitch to a platform and wait for the money to roll in, but campaigns need much more to succeed. There are now so many crowdsourcing campaigns that you need to invest a lot of effort (and cash) to stand out:

1. **Good presentation material:** With a choice of thousands of active campaigns, backers won't spend much time on each campaign before they choose. You'll need some very convincing material to get backers – this includes high-quality written material, pictures/illustrations and, most importantly, a good video. This will take a lot of your time, and you'll most likely need external consultants to make it.

2. **A marketing budget:** One of the biggest mistakes start-ups make is to think the platform does the work of driving backers to their campaigns – it doesn't. The start-up sends the majority of backers to the site, whether via its own extended network, PR activities, paid advertising (Facebook, Google, etc.) or other marketing activities. It can easily cost several thousand euros and hundreds of hours of your own time to draw attention to your campaign and sustain it for 30–60 days. The successful crowdfunding campaigns you hear about in the media are the result of a hard-working team that spent a lot of time and money on making the campaign a success!

3. **A plan for after the campaign has ended:** Your work doesn't finish with the end of a successful crowdfunding campaign. If you're in that lucky situation you will have several hundred backers to which you have promised to deliver a product sometime in the future. These can be great 'ambassadors' if you manage to keep good relationships with them in the months/years to come. But if they start believing that you won't live up to your promises, they can create a lot of hostility towards your company. To avoid this happening, you must not only deliver the product as intended, but also spend a lot of effort communicating with your backers via email or crowdfunding platforms. Many startups hire a part-time or full-time 'community manager' to handle this communication, which of course comes at a cost.

⚠ Key note: Remember to budget for crowdfunding costs

Christian Gabriel, CEO and founder of Capdesk, reminds founders to include the cost of running a crowdfunding campaign in their budget:

'Like any other marketing exercise, you can never spend enough money or time on your crowdfunding campaign. However, you can try to reverse-engineer your funding goal and try to control the figures as tightly as possible. The hardest job of any campaign is to get your "safe backers" to back you on the same day; arranging for 100 friends and family to buy the product within a few hours of each other is a hard exercise. To bring everything together, expect to take 1–3 months planning the campaign and have an additional budget of minimum $5,000 to figure out the graphics, copywriting and, most importantly, the video.'

• •

Could my startup raise money from reward-based crowdfunding?

Having considered the pros and cons of running a reward-based campaign, you also need to consider whether it is a realistic route for your startup. Before you launch a campaign, you should ask yourself if people would really pay you money up front for the development of your project. Assuming you have something exciting to show your backers, determining factors include:

1 customer base

2 affection, or empathy, for your campaign.

Customer base — B2B vs B2C

In general it's much harder to run successful reward-based crowdfunding campaigns for products and services aimed at business customers (B2B) than it is for consumer products (B2C). This is because the vast majority of potential backers on these platforms are consumers who invest in stuff they fall in love with, not something that might help a company. The chances of hundreds of decision-makers from a specific industry watching and deciding to fund your project are very slim.

Casper Arboll, a former crowdfunding professional at Heartreacher Crowd Consulting, explains why it's so difficult for B2B companies to raise money through crowdfunding:

'B2B products are underperforming in crowdfunding. The issue is that business needs are immediate and decision-making is free of emotions. No sensible procurement professional would spend company money to buy into a crowdfunding campaign where they risk never receiving the product; it's safer to buy an existing, more expensive and less innovative product. There is little comfort knowing you supported an entrepreneur-in-the-making if you put your job at risk. And consumers on reward-based crowdfunding platforms back products they are excited about and connect with – it could be a card game, a beer brand or a gadget. It's not very easy to be excited about an encryption module for compliance managers at big banks.'

Affection

Having a consumer product in the right phase is not enough to make your project suitable for reward-based crowdfunding. You need to capture the affection and attention of the backers, enough that they will be willing to spread the word among their network. Generally, backers feel affection for:

 © 2017 Nicolaj Højer Nielsen

A Your product: If you're asking people to pay up front for a product you haven't developed yet, which they might get in 12 months, they must really want the product! Of course, some products will generate more affection than others. Most people care more about the kind of computer or shoes they use than their toilet paper. This is also the reason why many projects within arts/music/fashion work well on reward platforms, since people have a lot more emotional involvement with products like these.

B Your mission: Ideally, backers feel affection not only for your product, but also for the mission you are on. This is because many backers on these platforms aren't just there to get 'cheap products'; they really want to support something that matters to them. This makes crowdfunding ideal for 'social entrepreneurship' projects, which many of the other funding sources don't support. As someone once said, 'It's not about what you do, but why you do it.'

C Your team: The people behind the product and the story you tell your backers play a hugely important role on crowdfunding platforms. Again, you're asking backers to pay for a product up front – quite a high risk with a very limited upside (normally a discount compared to the future price). So why do they do it, if we assume that they know the risk/reward? Because they want YOU to succeed! Therefore being able to describe your team and your mission and to tell this story in a short video will have a huge impact on your ability to raise money on a reward-based crowdfunding campaign.

Affection for your product + Empathy for your mission = Virality

Quite often, affection for your product and empathy for your mission leads to visitors and initial backers sharing your project with their network, primarily on social media and in traditional media, thereby giving the project a much-needed viral effect!

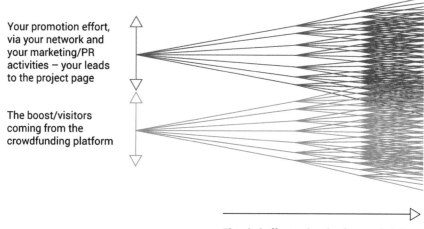

Your promotion effort, via your network and your marketing/PR activities – your leads to the project page

The boost/visitors coming from the crowdfunding platform

The viral effects when backers and visitors reshare info about your project on social media and offline

© 2017 Nicolaj Højer Nielsen

Without this virality, it's almost impossible to run a successful campaign. It's simply not possible to make it from your personal network and marketing efforts alone, even when you include the additional visitors/backers coming from the platform itself. You need the campaign to take on a life of its own.

Nothing happens unless you find the first 30% yourself

A very important rule of thumb for crowdfund campaigns is that they will be successful only if they reach approximately 30%+ of the funding goals very fast – i.e. within the first 1–2 days. If this happens, the campaign will be perceived as a success by both the platform's visitors (who'll then want to be part of the success) and the platform itself (which might feature it to give it more attention); and then the positive spiral and virality can begin.

Even with an inspirational concept and fantastic promotion material, it is virtually impossible for a campaign to get this much traction just by putting the project on the platform. YOU need to find the first 30% that want to invest, from your own network and/or pre-campaign marketing activities, and get them to 'buy' as soon as the campaign starts. Without this pre-marketing effort, there is a big risk that your campaign will be a failure owing to lack of early traction.

Running a reward-based crowdfunding campaign may seem cheap and easy from the outside, but it's the total opposite: it requires a lot of effort and cost to avoid being among the 65%+ of the launched crowdfunding campaigns who fail to reach their funding goals!

Case study: SOUNDBOKS – Start marketing months before launch

SOUNDBOKS is the world's most powerful battery-powered speaker, combining extreme volume, unbreakable design and long battery life; the company's vision is to enable anyone to throw a party, anywhere. The startup was founded with the original product in 2015 and by the beginning of 2016 SOUNDBOKS decided to launch the second version of the speaker through the crowdfunding platform Kickstarter.

SOUNDBOKS exceeded its funding goal in the first few hours of its Kickstarter campaign. The company's CMO Simon Kronenberg explains:

'In the preparation phase we interviewed a lot of successful campaigners. We were told that in order to have a successful campaign, you need to have significant traction from day

194 © 2017 Nicolaj Højer Nielsen

one. That's why we spent a lot of effort and resources building up a large email database of potential customers leading up to the campaign through a well-designed landing page and Facebook marketing campaign.'

Nick Traulsen of The Marketing Guy outlined his approach for the campaign:

'We knew that we could collect leads prior to the campaign, so while SOUNDBOKS worked on video, content and the Kickstarter page, we worked with a company called Lean Technologies, with the main focus being lead collection. We knew if we had enough emails we would be able to reach our goal with the emails alone. It was just a matter of how many it would take and what the cost of an email would be.

'We started collecting emails 2 or 3 months prior to the campaign and ended up developing a funnel that not only managed to keep the leads warm, but actually significantly increased trust in the team and the product.

'As the campaign launch date approached, we announced the date and time on the emails to make sure all the leads knew when we launched and made it very clear that they would have to be ready at that exact time to get the super early bird discount.

'Then we released around 10,000 emails at the time of the launch. Within 3 hours we reached our goal: $100,000 raised. That made it the fastest campaign to reach its goal in all of the Nordic countries. The campaign would go on to raise a total of $784,320 with much of the funds coming from those crucial leads. The fact that we reached the goal so early also helped other areas of the campaign. It ranked higher on Kickstarter, we got more PR and people tend to have higher trust in campaigns that are already funded.'

The 30% rule also goes for equity crowdfunding campaigns, which we will deal with in the section below.

Equity crowdfunding

While reward-based crowdfunding exchanges a product or other non-financial reward for funding, equity crowdfunding is where a startup sells equity in the company to the 'crowd'.

In the early stages of financing, equity is offered to a small number of family and friends or business angels in return for funding. In the case of equity crowdfunding, this equity is shared between a large number of small investors you don't know. The average investment size per investor in an equity crowdfunding campaign differs a lot between projects and from one platform to the next, but it's often in the range of €1,000–€2,000 per investor. This means that a startup that raises €500,000 will end up with 250–500 different shareholders at the end of the investment round.

Key note: Equity crowdfunding —Check with a local lawyer!

The legislation on equity crowdfunding is moving very fast! Most countries in the Western world are implementing new legislation to make equity crowdfunding legal, but progress and the requirements for legal crowdfunding campaigns vary from country to country. Therefore, check the current status with a local lawyer and your local financial authorities before launching an equity crowdfunding campaign!

How equity crowdfunding works

In theory, you could equity crowdfund your startup very easily: make a small website with your business plan and sell shares in your company for, say, €100 per share. Some startups do this, promoting their offer via paid advertising and social media, but most use equity crowdfunding platforms to market the investment opportunity to potential investors.

The table below includes some of the largest equity crowdfunding platforms in Europe:

Platform	Website	Country focus
SyndicateRoom	https://www.syndicateroom.com/	UK
CrowdCube	https://www.crowdcube.com/	UK
FundedByMe	https://www.fundedbyme.com/	Scandinavia
Invesdor	https://www.invesdor.com	Scandinavia
Seedmatch	https://www.seedmatch.de/	Germany
Seedrs	https://www.seedrs.com/	Europe-wide

The benefits of using an equity crowdfunding platform are:

1. You reach a wider audience by marketing your investment proposal on a known investment platform.

2. The fact that the opportunity is posted on the platform, and at least superficially screened by the platform, could reassure potential investors that it's safe to invest.

3. Administration and handling of investors can be easier, since you can use some of the platform's existing legal documents for the investment round, instead of having to handle the legalities on your own.

Of course, these platforms don't just support startups out of love; they are run as businesses. On average, platforms take approximately 6%–10% of the money you raise in commission.

· ·

(!) **Key note: Investigate the legal differences before you choose an equity crowdfunding platform**

You need to investigate thoroughly before you decide which equity platform to use. The platforms are very different, not only in their geographical focus areas but also in the legal structure of the equity crowdfunding campaigns.

With some platforms, the crowd investors become direct shareholders in your company (meaning you then have to manage several hundred shareholders), while other platforms allow you to create a single investment company that the crowd investors can invest into (which can ease administration) and still other platforms act as a nominee for the crowd investors (which can ease administration further, but of course comes at a cost). Which one you should choose depends on your specific needs, so investigate the pros and cons of the different models/platforms before signing up!

· ·

What and when to equity crowdfund

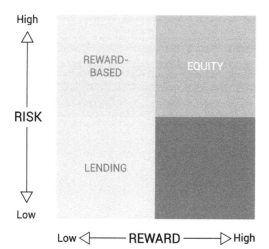

There's a big difference between reward-based crowdfunding and equity crowdfunding. Reward crowdfunders' primary reason is to support the project, since an upfront 'investment' to get a product much later makes little financial sense. Equity crowdfunding is different, at least in theory, because the investors are hoping for financial gain.

It is mainly high risk/high reward projects that are equity crowdfunded. This is owing to the fact that the crowdfunders are private individuals who aren't investing solely for financial gain; they're also looking for the excitement of being a shareholder in something fun that could potentially be 'the next big thing'. Unlike reward-based crowdfunding, it would be very hard to equity crowdfund a high risk/low reward project.

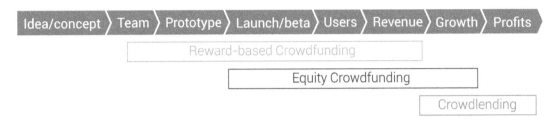

This also means it's not possible to equity crowdfund an 'undeveloped business idea', since this is always a high risk/low reward project. Exceptions exist, but as a general rule you will need to demonstrate some traction before investors will buy shares in the company. As platforms tend to select cases with higher chances of a successful campaign, it is unlikely that an undeveloped idea will be able to even start an equity crowdfunding campaign unless it goes it alone.

 Key note: Equity crowdfunding is not your first funding source!

Equity crowdfunding is typically NOT the first investor in your company. You can consider equity crowdfunding at approximately the same stage as when business angels would be interested in your project, i.e. after you have gathered a competent team, developed the first prototype and maybe even had some revenue and/or users. Before that you should look for alternative sources of funding.

 © 2017 Nicolaj Højer Nielsen

Who invests in equity crowdfunding?

So who does invest in equity crowdfunding? Capdesk, a company that helps equity crowd-funded companies organise shareholding, has some interesting findings regarding who funds equity crowdfunding campaigns. According to Capdesk, investors come from three sources:

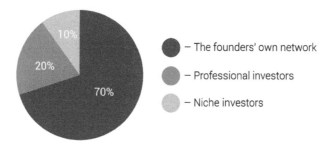

A company's own network includes team members, existing investors, existing customers, friends, colleagues and family. These investors represent on average 70% of the total campaign. Professional investors find the campaign through the investment platform. These are investors who are good at evaluating cases and often invest larger sums through tax schemes, like the SEIS and the EIS in the UK. Niche investors also find the campaign through the platform. These invest primarily because of a passion for the product, solution or team. They may be professional investors (e.g. a business angel giving €1,000 just to show support) or non-accredited investors who might not understand the offering but want to be part of the company.

This is a big surprise for most entrepreneurs the first time they do equity crowdfunding: they often believe that the majority of the backers will be found via the platform and they are not aware that companies have to bring the vast majority of the backers themselves!

Case study: Solar for Schools – Be prepared to spend a month fundraising yourself

Solar for Schools is a UK-based social enterprise bringing investors and schools together to raise money to install solar panels on school roofs. The company turned to equity crowdfunding after an initial friends and family round of £160,000.

The campaign exceeded its £400,000 target, but got off to a slow start owing to a lack of initial support. CEO Robert Schrimpff explains:

'We liked the idea of equity crowdfunding because, given the nature of the business, we felt having a broad base of shareholders who could act as ambassadors and also then invest in the solar assets themselves would help the company grow faster. I could have raised the money from a few angels but I wanted to cast the net wider.

'We did achieve our target – in fact, we shot past it in the last couple of days – but it was incredibly hard work. Unfortunately, I underestimated the effort required to provide all the evidence for due diligence and had some legal and tax issues to deal with, so I had no time for pre-marketing.

'Luckily I had structured a bridge round in two parts, where the second part was via the platform, so I had 15% of the round "secured" before starting and quickly doubled that through my own network in the first 2 weeks. Up until that point many were following but virtually nobody was investing.

'I started to realise that for risky equity investments, the crowd only follows a crowd. You need to have critical mass. Once we hit target, hundreds of them tried to invest 50–500 pounds!

'I decided I needed to get to at least 200k for the crowd to follow. I spent my weekends emailing friends and acquaintances, posting on Facebook, Twitter and various mailing lists I'm a member of. I must have sent over 10,000 emails to over 3,000 people. I also called dozens of them and met with a few. Towards the end, I really focused on people I felt could actually write a large cheque and who understood the industry. In the end, most of our investors were either successful entrepreneurs in the Internet or solar space, or partners in infrastructure funds who invested personally.

'I'd advise anyone considering equity crowdfunding to start telling their network a week or two before the launch and build a team of social media ambassadors who'll retweet and post your messages during the campaign. Be prepared to spend a month fundraising yourself anyway. Think of the platform as the clock and the supporting website, not the solution to your fundraising problems.'

As equity crowdfunders are not necessarily professional investors, it can be very hard to determine which projects will be funded before a campaign starts. Projects that seem like good investment opportunities may not do well on a crowdfunding platform, while other projects (which professional investors don't find that interesting) will often exceed their goals.

This is mainly owing to three things that make equity crowdfunders different from more professional investors:

1. **They are not experts:** Most business angels and venture capitalists invest in areas they know quite a bit about. These most often say no to investment opportunities

 © 2017 Nicolaj Højer Nielsen

outside their expert field. People visiting equity crowdfunding sites most often ARE NOT experts and happily invest in areas they know relatively little about.

2 **They invest limited money.** Equity crowdfunders invest only a limited amount of money per startup, with an average 'micro-investment' on most platforms of €1,000–€4,000 per investor per project.

3 **They dedicate limited time:** Everyone can become an expert in a subject if they spend enough time. But with small investments it makes little sense to dedicate days of research into a company. Studies show that the average equity crowdfunding investor takes only a few minutes before deciding to invest!

- -

⚠ Key note: Equity crowdfunding doesn't validate your business in the minds of professional investors

Unlike reward-based crowdfunding, which gives a clear indication of public demand for your product, equity crowdfunding won't reassure professional investors in the same way. Professional investors know that most of your equity crowdfunding comes from investors who are not experts and who have not carried out detailed due diligence on your business. This means that equity crowdfunding does not validate your business in the eyes of angel or VC investors.

- -

What does this mean for startups wanting to do equity crowdfunding?

1 **B2B startups are harder, but not impossible, to do equity crowdfunding for.** Because many equity crowdfunders are inexperienced investors, B2B startups are harder to fund than the average B2C startup. However, equity crowdfunding does draw some professional investors, so B2B startups that have progressed long enough to show impressive growth in users/revenue may be able to convince equity crowdfunders to invest.

2 **Your online pitch is everything!** Most business angels will persevere with a lousy pitch deck, since they tend to spend much longer evaluating the business opportunity (especially if being introduced to it via a trusted contact). Equity crowdfunders take just a few minutes to decide whether to invest or move on, so the pitch material (especially the video on the platform) is everything.

3 **Set a low fundraising goal:** As with reward crowdfunding, you need to set a fundraising goal that you're sure to get. Some platforms only pay out the investments if you reach 100% of your pre-set funding goal, though this is more to make sure you look like a success. When you are close to reaching your funding goal, the platform will most likely feature you and your 'success' will create further interest from equity crowdfunders that jump on the bandwagon.

Case study: Virtuous Vodka – Small investors won't work for you

Virtuous Vodka is a Swedish company selling naturally flavoured vodkas. The company started in early 2012 and, after an initial friends and family round, turned to equity crowdfunding to raise SEK1 million in the first year and SEK2 million in 2014.

Partner and chairman Johan Ranstam explains:

'We initially only planned on running a crowd-financed release party for the vodka, but on our way to the meeting we discussed our funding and the alternatives we had. We thought it would be fun to see if people would be willing to buy equity in the vodka company, since it would be a nice thing for people to "brag" about.

'With the first funding round, there was nothing to offer in terms of product or revenue (the product hit the shelves in May 2013). In the first round we raised SEK1 million in return for 9.99% of the company's shares.

'After covering production costs, our main concern for the first crowdfunding round was to gain ambassadors for the product and we were very successful at that. The campaign was easy. We got lots of attention and collected the full amount in just shy of 3 weeks. It was a blast!

'The second round was a lot more about equity for expansion and less about marketing, but it didn't go well. We opted for crowdfunding as a matter of convenience – we already had the connections and expected everything to go as easy as before. But this time everything was wrong. We weren't as invested in PR as the first time, and the platform pushed the campaign forward so the timing was out.

'We wanted SEK6–8 million for sales and marketing and had a back-up plan of SEK3 million, but we only raised SEK2 million. This was enough to keep the company going, but didn't leave anything but scrap money for expansion.

'Currently the company has 360 investors, of which approximately 300 are crowdfunders. We have done one further round with angels and current investors to fund the much-desired expansion.

'Equity crowdfunding hasn't actually been any problem at all, but not the boost that we hoped for and expected. Generally I'd say that an investment of a couple of thousand SEK won't make people work for you.'

 © 2017 Nicolaj Højer Nielsen

Crowdlending

The third major way to crowdfund your startup is via crowdlending. This method raises a loan for your startup, but, unlike the traditional method of raising a loan from your bank, the loan comes from many small lenders, who are most often private individuals.

So why should you go to many small lenders instead of a regular bank? Because banks, as you have read in this chapter, don't lend money to startups! Banks lend money only after a few years of showing profits, by which time you're not really a startup anymore.

Via crowdlending, startups can access loans significantly earlier than via the banks. Businesses turning to crowdlending typically raise loans in the range of €50,000–€500,000, spread over hundreds of lenders.

How to get a crowdloan

Unlike equity crowdfunding, crowdlending in most countries is not under the same tight financial regulation, so any startup could reach out to its network and try to syndicate loans from, say, 100 different lenders. However, since most people don't have that kind of network and the paperwork required to manage hundreds of loan documents can be enormous, most crowdlending takes place via dedicated crowdlending platforms.

The leading crowdlending platforms in Europe are:

Platform	Website	Country focus
Zopa	http://www.zopa.com/	UK/US
Funding Circle	https://www.fundingcircle.com/uk/	UK only
Lendix	https://lendix.com/	France
AuxMoney	https://www.auxmoney.com/	Germany
isePankur	https://www.isepankur.ee/home	Europe-wide
Lendino	https://www.lendino.dk/	Denmark

Lending platforms divide the loan opportunities into different categories, with different levels of interest rates to be paid depending on the perceived risk. They then market these loan opportunities to the potential lenders. If the offer generates enough interest, the loan is created, contracts are signed and money is transferred to the company.

The table below illustrates the current (March 2017) interest rates for companies seeking crowdlending via Funding Circle. The interest rate paid depends on the perceived riskiness of the company borrowing the money (categorised in Funding Circle from the safest companies, rated A+, to the riskiest category, E) and also the length of the loan.

Term	A+	A	B	C	D	E
6 months	4.9%	7.0%	8.5%	11.0%	14.9%	17.9%
12 months	5.5%	7.5%	9.0%	11.5%	15.5%	18.9%
24 months	6.5%	8.0%	9.5%	12.5%	15.9%	19.9%
36 months	6.5%	8.5%	10.0%	12.5%	16.9%	20.9%
48 months	7.0%	9.0%	10.5%	12.9%	17.5%	21.5%
60 months	7.5%	9.0%	10.5%	13.5%	17.9%	21.9%

Source: FundingCircle.com

The business model of most crowdlending platforms is quite similar: in addition to the interest paid from the company to the lenders, the platform receives a one-time fee for securing the loan and an additional interest margin (typically in the range of 1%) for handling the payments from the company to the lenders.

Case study: Early Bird – Crowdlending is easier and faster to use than the bank

Once a crowdlending campaign is in place, the funding can be raised extremely quickly. Danish startup Early Bird turned to crowdlending when it was ready to expand its business abroad. Co-founder Martin Aleth describes its experience:

'Myself and my partner Brian Köster founded Early Bird in 2011. The company uses a cloud-based platform to sell last-minute restaurant bookings at a discounted price. Initially, the company grew organically (bootstrapped and via a small credit line at the bank) until 2015 when we decided to run a crowdlending campaign on the platform Lendino.

'By then, we had 5,000 people dining per month and were established on the Danish market with a positive cash-flow despite continuously investing in IT and marketing.

 © 2017 Nicolaj Højer Nielsen

We decided to run the campaign because we wanted to go abroad, but we needed liquidity to invest in a franchise setup (lawyers, consultancies, international trademarks and domains).

'We considered all the options, but crowdlending suited us best. The bank required a lot of documentation and wasn't so positive about lending us more money. We didn't want to risk relationships with our friends and family, and we didn't want to give up control of our business to investors. The business had already proved positive in economic terms, so we just made a plan for paying back the loan.

'We asked to raise DKK300,000, which the platform approved after it assessed our financial statements and historical performance. After that it made a risk assessment and set an interest rate of 7% p.a. with a fee of 1% p.a. for the platform on top of that. For its fee, Lendino did all the marketing – we didn't know any of the backers ourselves.

'One thing that has surprised us about crowdlending is the way the broad public think about lending money. Because of the media hype of new investments, the public generally think money from investors is a signal of success and a loan is because the business is going bad. This may be because people can relate to this from their personal economy.

'This is obviously not true for everyone, because the loan was backed within 24 hours. We had 47 backers, who invested between DKK1,000 and DKK80,000.

'I would recommend crowdlending to all entrepreneurs. We have been very satisfied with the platform, which was easier and faster to use than the bank. It was really easy to sign up on the website and a very transparent marketplace. Just make sure that you have the economy to pay back the loan and everything will be fine.'

When and what to crowdlend

Crowdlending is different from other types of crowdfunding in that there is no upside for the 'backers' other than the interest on the loan. With equity crowdfunding the backers have a chance of being part of the next Instagram or Google and earning millions, but with crowdlending the company only pays back the loan, with no further financial upside (although you can reward backers by allowing them to be the first to get the product – often at a discount).

So what does this mean for companies considering crowdlending?

The bad news first: you can only crowdlend when you have a stable cash-flow! Given the high risk, early-stage startups are not suited for crowdlending. This funding source only makes sense AFTER you have proven your business. Most crowdlending platforms require you to provide annual reports for at least the last 2–3 years, to prove your ability to make money (and thereby repay your loan) and generate a stable cash-flow.

The good news: you can also crowdlend B2B projects. With crowdlending, not having a B2C business is not a disadvantage! In fact, many platforms and their lenders like B2B projects, since it's often easier to evaluate the business risk and potential of a B2B project, unlike a product that claims to be the next SnapChat. So crowdlending is a very realistic funding source for a B2B company that has already proven its business.

Take-away points

Crowdfunding is one of the more hyped areas of startup funding since it can provide startups with many alternative funding routes. But in fact crowdfunding is a word that describes three very different ways to get funded: reward-based crowdfunding, where you pre-sell your project; equity crowdfunding, where you sell shares in your startup; and crowdlending, where the crowd provides your startup with micro-loans.

For early-stage startups, reward-based crowdfunding is the most relevant, since equity crowdfunding can be considered only when you achieve traction, and lending is not possible until you have a stable cash-flow.

But you can't crowdfund all projects! Since most investors are private persons who are backing for non-financial reasons, projects that excite them have the biggest chance of success. This also means that it's very hard to crowdfund B2B projects.

Even if you have a project that might be relevant for crowdfunding, you must also be aware that the majority of the backers/investors do NOT come from the platform itself, but from the people you draw to the platform via your own network and/or marketing. This means that running a successful crowdfunding campaign is as much hard work as raising money from other sources!

 © 2017 Nicolaj Højer Nielsen

© 2017 Nicolaj Højer Nielsen

Chapter 13

How to contact investors

We have reached the point when the startup is ready to initiate contact and dialogue with potential investors. At this point it's important to understand how to go about that initial contact and to know what materials investors expect to see.

A common mistake is for entrepreneurs to send their 50-page business plan to 30-something investors and then sit back waiting for them to call and invite them to pitch. But before you send out any material, you need to get the trust of a potential investor. They get hundreds, if not thousands, of contact requests a year. Every entrepreneur thinks they have the best idea or they wouldn't be doing it. But why should a busy, time-strapped investor speak to you? What's in it for them?

In this chapter you will learn how to approach potential investors, and why you shouldn't send them a business plan.

Rule number 1 – Don't write a business plan!

Many entrepreneurs believe they should write a long and well-articulated business plan, setting out in detail all their future plans, and that the business plan is key to funding.

Wrong. If you send a long business plan to a professional investor I can guarantee they won't read it – and for three reasons:

1. It's too long
2. It's full of irrelevant details
3. It's out of date

1. Too long

Investors won't allocate time to read a 50-page business plan, especially not early in the process when they're mainly looking to weed out unsuitable opportunities. They get so many opportunities that they must be able to evaluate yours in three or four pages. If you send them a long business plan, they might read the first five pages to see if it has an executive summary and they won't read the rest.

Danish venture capitalist Nikolaj Nyholm works as a partner in Sunstone Capital. I once asked him what he does when an unsolicited, long business plan is emailed to him. He said, 'It will most likely rot to death in my inbox.'

 © 2017 Nicolaj Højer Nielsen

2. Irrelevant details

A business plan is often full of irrelevant information. When you write it, you're caught up in explaining a lot of details about the future – many of these are of limited interest and value to a potential investor. When you try to estimate your rental costs in three years, or whether in five years you'll go into other territories like Germany before Spain, you will lose them. They know the plan will change many times before then.

What investors are looking for are specific elements of the business model: the problem you're solving, how you're solving it, who your customers are, the team, etc. They don't want to play the needle in the haystack game, trying to locate those five or 10 useful pages among dozens.

3. Outdated

The problem with a lengthy and detailed plan, with graphs of your cost of business and your market penetration guesstimates for year five, is that it's outdated as soon as you press the print button. Perhaps you assume that your customers will pay €10 and they'll be in Europe, and then you launch and find out that the customers won't pay €10 and they come from Asia. That changes the entire plan, revenues, costs and how you market your product.

 Key note: A business plan is seen as a negative signal

If I see a hundred page business plan from a founder, I think, 'They're sitting and spending three months in the basement making this perfect plan instead of going out and talking to customers or making the product.' That says something about how they think about entrepreneurship and how to get started. Perhaps they have their reasons for doing so, but to me it signals that their priorities are off.

Just ask the founders of some of the most successful startups what their initial business idea was, and you'll find it was very different from the business they are running now. Investors know that and therefore won't spend hours reading your lengthy plan.

 Key note: What to do instead of creating a long business plan

You need to focus on two things instead of creating a formal business plan:

1. **Process.** You need an agile process, getting you from your idea to closer to a real business. I recommend reading books like *The Lean Startup* and *Running Lean*. By reading these books you can learn to apply important concepts for agile development, like minimum viable product, build-measure-learn, and business model canvas/lean canvas.

2. **Material.** Read Chapter 13 for the material you should develop and use in communication with your potential investors – this doesn't include a business plan!

Should you ever make plan for internal use?

Should you write a business plan just for internal use? Most serial entrepreneurs acknowledge that there's real value in planning and thinking about the future, in thinking about what they really want to achieve and how they want to solve a problem. Winston Churchill famously said, '*Plans are of little importance, but planning is essential.*'

The value for me and most serial entrepreneurs is not the business plan as a document, but rather the process of making it. You and your co-founder(s) will learn a lot from discussing the really important subjects about the business; the where, what, how, who, why, and when. What you find will have important implications both for your business and for your funding strategy.

Planning and strategizing is essential for determining and aligning you and your team to where you want to go. The question is: what is the best process for you internally to get that alignment? Is that a business plan or is it a different kind of process? My opinion (which is echoed by many investors and serial entrepreneurs) is that you need a more agile process and documentation than the classic business plan approach offers.

(!) Key note: What do you do if an investor asks you to send a business plan?

Some investors will *ask* for business plan. If this is the case, you should decode what they're asking for. The investor doesn't want a hundred page Word document; what they want is to understand your business. Your investor slide-deck and budget should be linked and are normally enough for an investor to decide to take the next step with you. If they ask for more, you should ask the investor what specific information they would like to see. Then you can update your investor slide-deck accordingly. You might find all the investors you approach ask for the same five or 10 extra pages. If so, add them to your main slide-deck and this will become your business plan.

 © 2017 Nicolaj Højer Nielsen

Rule number 2 – Trust is the most important factor

I know I'm repeating myself, but it's important: trust is the most important factor.

For any investor to invest in a startup, they need to have a lot of trust given the scary statistics on how many startups fail. You can even divide this trust into two things the investor must believe in: trust in the business opportunity (that the problem you are trying to solve is real, that the market is big enough etc.), and trust in your team (that you have what it takes to deliver on the opportunity).

But there is a big difference between early- and late-stage startups when it comes to how trust is generated.

If you're a late stage startup, you have a product, users, paying customers and revenue, and a team that have delivered the above. What this means is you have a lot of historic data, that is both quantitative and qualitative, to support your claims. You are able to provide credible answers to tough questions like: *What is the cost of getting a customer? How much are they willing to pay?* and *How big is the market?* Real data beats every scenario analysis there is. If you have customers paying, that is proof – and proof generates trust. Of course, they still have to have trust in you and the team, but it's relatively easy to convince investors about the business because you have real data.

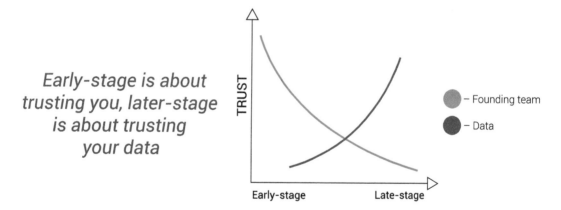

Early-stage is about trusting you, later-stage is about trusting your data

But what about an early-stage startup? You might have a beta version of the product, maybe you have some users, but you probably don't have paying customers yet. You've hopefully convinced a few people to join you, but it's likely to be an incomplete team. You have very little performance data; it's all about the future. You're saying, 'I *think* there's a big market; I *think* my customer would pay for this cool product if I made it.'

© 2017 Nicolaj Højer Nielsen

Key note: Focus on you and not the market

For later stage investing, even if the investor doesn't trust you, the figures don't lie, and investors put their trust in the data, but in early-stage investing, it is even more about trust in you.

Early-stage startups should of course explain the business and market opportunity, but it's really 80 per cent about you and 20 per cent about the business.

VC explains: Personal trust is local

Arne Tonning is partner at the venture capital fund Alliance Venture and explains why startups need to understand that early-stage financing is local:

The probability of investment is inversely proportional to the distance between the founder(s) and investor.

Early-stage investment is still a local business to the extent that it's more likely an investor is located close to the founder(s)/startups. For early-stage investments, relationships and access to references on a personal level is a critical factor for de-risking a case for investors in the absence of the clear business metrics that are more present in later stages. Your credibility as a founder is highly dependent on your personal network: where you worked, where you studied, etc. This is hard to replicate for someone 'alien'.

While it's difficult, factors such as relocating, building common networks, or at least having a very specific expertise in common with an investor may help reduce the perceived distance between a founder and an investor, thus making an investment more likely. This can take time. The quickest way to gain 'locality' quickly is by going through the best accelerator programs. However, fundraising closer to home is in my view more likely to be a successful path for most startups at the starting point.

 © 2017 Nicolaj Højer Nielsen

How do you get investors to trust you?

If it's all about trust, how do you get early-stage investors to trust you? There are two different types of investors: those you already know, and the rest. Perhaps you have an acquaintance, or friends and family, who know you and have the means to invest in you. Great, they know you and therefore trust you (and, if they don't trust you, perhaps you should look in the mirror).

Most startups will have to go beyond their personal network and approach investors they don't know at some point. When they do, they will need to build trust.

The key point here is that trust is built over time. You're unlikely to trust a person you have met for half an hour. This explains why you can't expect to get the money on the same day you meet a potential investor – there's no personal trust. Even if they think you're cool, feel you have what it takes, and you have a great business, the chance you'll get money the same day or the day after you meet is tiny.

We discussed earlier that the process televised on the show *Dragon's Den/Shark Tank* is fake. It's a theatre where you pitch in front of five investors, they discuss what you've said and then say, 'OK, we'll invest two hundred thousand euros'. In reality this never happens.

Entrepreneur turned venture capitalist, Mark Suster, from Both Sides of The Table, said, *I don't invest in a dot, I invest in a line.*

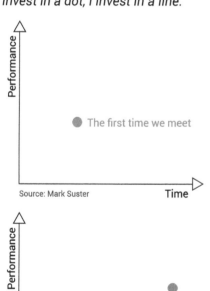

Source: Mark Suster

Imagine yourself as a dot on a graph with performance on the y versus time on the x. Even if your performance at a given time is good, investors want to see a line so they can see you at different points in time. Investors look at entrepreneurs they heard about six months ago who had great plans for the future, and when they meet six months later they may see they're still not quite there yet but the line is going in the right direction.

As Lars Andersen, General Partner in SEED Capital, explains:

The most common mistake startups make in relation to contacting VCs is that they make contact too late. Seriously, it's about sticking your neck out there. Your product doesn't have to be perfect. Build a minimum viable product, use it to learn about your customers, and start contacting VCs. We might say that it's still too early, but that doesn't mean never. The now successful wine scanner app, Vivino, had a first product that was absolute crap, but they gave us something to work from. This creates a paradox for many startups.

You should not count on VC money too early since in reality they invest rather late in the process, but you need to begin building relationships with them early on. They need time to get to know you before they invest their money – just make sure you don't waste too much time on coffee with VC partners!

 Key note: Build relationships with investors ahead of time!

What does this mean to startups? You have to build relationships with potential investors before you need the money – you shouldn't wait until you have everything in place. Create relationships now.

How do you build relationships with potential investors?

There are three important points to keep in mind when reaching out to investors:

How to contact potential investors

Get introduced by mutual contacts

Investors are generally short of time, but opportunity rich. They have lots of opportunities presented to them, but little time to evaluate them. They have to prioritise – it's like a business sales funnel. Out of the thousands of entrepreneurs who knock on their door each year, they might invest in one to five. They'll spend a lot of time with those selected entrepreneurs. As an early-stage investor, they have to be careful not to take two or three hundred down the sales funnel because they can't go into depth with that number. They need to say yes or no quickly, find the 30 or 50 to take to the next stage (a meeting), and then find the one to five they want to invest in.

 © 2017 Nicolaj Højer Nielsen

Even if they wanted to, they can't meet everyone who contacts them, so they have to say no to a lot of requests. So, although they're not just deleting emails without reading them, they might spend just 10 seconds on each message. Ten seconds!

Advice from former VC: The biggest mistake from startups when contacting VCs

Søren Jessen Nielsen (former general partner of two venture capital funds).

The biggest mistake made by entrepreneurs when searching for venture capital is to send unsolicited emails to a given VC fund. A VC partner rarely spends that much time on such emails, simply because there are so many startups contacting them. A given VC partner might have over 500 companies contacting them a year, so saying no early in the process is a way to manage their time. They may skim the email, but are unlikely to spend too much time on it and the chance of it leading to a meeting is very low. Compare this to a case in which the partner is introduced to the startup via a mutual contact; the partner will evaluate this request in much more detail. Ideally, it will come from an experienced/known business angel, and in the dream scenario the business angel will indicate they are interested in investing in the startup.

You should avoid spending time on cold-emailing VC partners, and instead spend your time on building relationships with people who can introduce you to the right partners!

In 2015, I reached out to a number of potential investors (venture capital funds) in Silicon Valley for one of my ventures. Despite only contacting investors who were active in the specific subfield, it was almost impossible to book meetings, or even get feedback on emails, from most of the funds I contacted. But when I was introduced via a mutual contact to the same partners in the same funds, almost all of them responded instantly, resulting in lots of investment meetings. Why? Because they took the time to read my email and take it seriously as it was now associated with a trusted contact.

Key note: You need introductions!

If you want to get in contact with an investor, it's crucial to get introduced by a mutual contact, someone who can vouch for you and who knows the investor well enough to make the introduction count. The person making the introduction is saying: 'I trust them; take it from here.' It's basic business sense: your mutual contact is establishing trust for the investor to take you seriously.

Below is an example of an introductory email I used when I wanted to get in contact with a US-based venture fund. I connected them via a good friend of mine who already knew the partner at the specific venture fund and was in a position to make an introduction.

From: **Dan Eisenhardt** ▓▓▓▓▓▓▓▓▓▓▓▓▓
Date: 2015-05-27 21:26 GMT+02:00
Subject: Intro to Sepior
To: ▓▓▓▓▓▓▓▓▓▓▓▓
Cc: ▓▓▓▓▓▓▓

Hi ▓▓▓

Hope things are going well at ▓▓▓▓▓

I want to introduce Nicolaj H Nielsen, who is a Danish serial entrepreneur and also one of the first investors in Recon Instruments. He is co-founder of Sepior, that is a startup working in the cloud encryption space. Sepior is currently headquuarted in Denmark, where it has received seed funding, but is now investigating a potential move of HQ to US (but keep R&D in Denmark). Nicolaj is looking for the right point of entry into ▓▓▓▓▓ since Sepior might be a right fit for either ▓▓▓▓▓ directly or for the dedicated ▓▓ fund you have created. Nicolaj and the CTO of Sepior will be in Bay area next week.

Please find attached a brief intro deck on Sepior.

Best regards,

Dan

Dan Eisenhardt
President & CEO

recon
INSTRUMENTS

Join groups, ask for referrals, look for venture capitalists online and then ask your networks for referrals. Don't cold call. They probably invest in less than one per cent of the companies they look at so you need to get a foot in the door.

You need to find contacts to introduce you to the right partners in the right funds in your country. That's not to say they'll invest straight away, but you'll gain their initial trust. Then you need to build on that trust and show you have a cool team, you know what you're doing, you have a product that is much better, a business model that is scalable, and the market you are building is big.

Do your research and contact the right investors

Though you may not need funding right now, you shouldn't spend time contacting investors that are likely wrong for you – and you shouldn't waste their time either. You need to find investors who are relevant and who invest in:

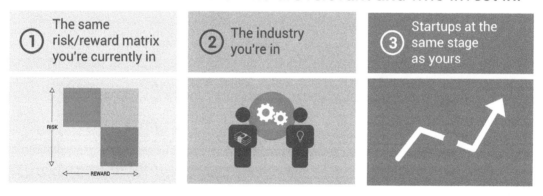

You need to find investors who are relevant and who invest in:

1. The same risk/reward matrix you're currently in
2. The industry you're in
3. Startups at the same stage as yours

If you're an early-stage startup and barely off the ground, you shouldn't contact investors who normally invest hundreds of millions of euros. Those hundred million euros implies they invest very late, and your startup is therefore not relevant to them – neither now, or 12 months from now.

When you've done your research and located a relevant investor, find a mutual contact who can introduce you to them. A good reason you should focus on relevant investors alone is because you will need an introduction. Imagine I'm a mutual contact and you ask me to introduce you to an investor. If I later find out your startup isn't relevant to that investor, I will end up looking bad for having introduced you.

Be specific

You've found a particular investor who you'd like to talk to and ask for advice because you want money at some point in the future and therefore want to start building a relationship now. You need to be very specific in your request for a meeting. Remember, investors get many requests for such meetings every day.

Business angel: Don't just ask for coffee!

Tommy Andersen, a tech entrepreneur and business angel, explains:

The biggest mistake startups make when pitching to me is saying, 'Let's have a coffee' without even telling me why. I have a busy daily routine and meet a lot of start-ups and founders all the time. Therefore, pitch me with a clear call-to-action and a clear message why we should meet for that special coffee. Just asking for a meet-up to hear about the world's greatest idea doesn't do the trick.

When you contact an investor you have to be specific about why the investor should take time out to meet you. Is it because you need the money now? Is it because you need some kind of advice? Maybe your questions can be answered by a phone call? Even when investors reduce the thousands of requests to a few hundred that seem relevant, that's still a lot of meetings. Make the investor's life easier by being specific.

When I get contacted by people who aren't specific, I write back and tell them to call me. That way, I achieve two things: it's much more time efficient for me because in a 10 minute call I can give some useful advice, and more than 50 per cent never call which maybe even more important. If an entrepreneur doesn't have the guts to call a potential investor or adviser when asked to do so, that's a firm indication they don't have what it takes to succeed.

 © 2017 Nicolaj Højer Nielsen

Take-away points

Don't write a long business plan for investors. It will most likely not be read because it's too detailed at this point and will be full of irrelevant information based on very high level assumptions and outdated as soon as you hit 'send'. Three to four pages should be enough to say everything they need to know.

Investing in early-stage startups is all about trust; particularly personal trust in you and your team. Ideally you know the person already, otherwise use your contacts to get a great introduction to the right investors who are in the right market.

Building trust is essential, and takes time to build. Therefore reach out to the potential investors ahead of time and not at the last minute!

Chapter 14:
Guide to investor material

Getting an investor is a process. In this chapter we will look at the different types of material you need to produce for each step in the funding process. What do you need to bring? What data/material is the investor expecting to see?

It's similar to hunting for a new job. You have to find an open position, contact them, send the correct information, and present it to them. You might need to provide references or further information. Finally, you sign a contract.

Getting financing is no different. Your goal with the first application is (as with your first contact with a potential employer) is not to get the job, it's to get to the next step in the process – the interview. You need different material for different steps.

Step 1 – The first contact

The best way for you to get introduced to a potential investor is through a mutual contact. But even then, you shouldn't wait for the potential investor to get back to you. You need to take the first step.

This first step is typically via phone or email. The goal is to generate interest: an invitation to drop by for a presentation or a request for more information. You want the investor to be so interested in your proposal that they select you as one of the proposals they will spend more time evaluating. Question is, how do you generate that interest?

I propose that your email (or pitch over the phone) contains the following three elements:

1. Firstly, make it clear why your case is interesting for them. Quickly state that it's something that fits with what they invest in, that it is at the right stage for them, and that the industry risk/reward position is similar to what they're looking for. To do this effectively you need to do some desk research before contacting the investor, to find out what they are interested in.

2. Secondly, give strong cues to your personal credibility, for example, what you've done in the past, your education, the companies you've worked for, and other startups you've been involved with. This also involves name-dropping the person who introduced you to the investor or other mutual contacts who can further strengthen your credibility.

3. Finally, tell them what you want to do next: ask for permission to send them more information or request a meeting with them.

First contact example email

Below is an example of a first contact email sent out from me in 2009 to potential investors (business angels) in Recon Instruments.

 © 2017 Nicolaj Højer Nielsen

██████████,

My name is Nicolaj Nielsen, and I'm an INSEAD graduate (MBA'06J).

I am contacting you because I since 2008 have invested my personal funds as seed capital for a start-up called Recon Instruments (www.reconinstruments.com) and because you in the INSEAD Alumni database have indicated an interest in **angel investments**.

Recon Instruments is the first company in the world to integrate a Head Mounted Display into a pair of ski goggles. Using embedded state-of-the-art sensor and GPS technology we provide easy access to navigation, communication, and performance based-information in real time. We consider ourselves the Intel Inside of the action sports industry, partnering with well known brands and distributors to bring our electronics and optics to consumers and professional athletes alike.

We are currently partnering with a high-end Goggle and Sunglasses brand for an exclusive September 2010 launch in North America and Europe. The Recon Alpine Goggle's feature set includes: speed, altimeter, vertical odometer, stop-watch, temperature, and time. These performance statistics can be viewed in real-time or après-ski. Content can be uploaded via USB to your PC and shared online. Future models include seamless integration to I-Phone/Smartphone, Hands-free interfacing using gesture control, and camera integrated solutions enabling recording and viewing of video content during an activity. I have attached a picture of the first product (ski-goggle).

Founded in 2006, incorporated in 2008, Recon Instruments is a privately-held company with just fewer than twenty employees. With offices in Vancouver and boundless testing grounds in Whistler, home of the 2010 winter Olympics, Recon Instruments is dedicated to enhancing performance and experience of millions of action sports enthusiast around the world. We are already endorsed by a growing community of alpine skiers and snowboarders and we are in the final as the hottest new brand of 2010 at ISPO in Europe. In January we are shooting a film with Discovery Channel to be aired during Olympics.

We are raising CAD 0.9-1.5 million in an Angel round to finance the scale up to mass production and to fuel the growth into related industry applications (other action sports, aircraft, military). Just under $1 million has been raised to date, with 50% government funding rate, so we are firmly positioned to provide significant leverage on each dollar invested and thus expect a 10 times return multiplier in 3-4 years through either cash buyout or IPO. The closest industry comparable is a Public company named Microvision trading at 64x revenues, which confirms the market's belief in the future of Head Mounted Display technologies.

We are already now getting massive PR, even though the first product will not be showcased until a major tradeshow in Denver in January:

- + 100,000 web page hits first two weeks of December 2009
- Pre-order requests coming in at 50-100/day
- Featured in over 100 web articles around the world
- Request from CBS, Fox, and many other media providers
- Partnership web requests from hundreds of tech companies, retailers, and distributors around the world

Please reply to this email if you are interested in learning more about the investment opportunity. We will be sure to respond promptly with an executive summary for your perusal.

Best regards,

Nicolaj H. Nielsen

Of course, this isn't a perfect email, but it's a real email that got results. Let's look at it in detail.

This email was sent out to people in my alumni, people I went to MBA school with, so the subject line includes the school name (INSEAD) which gives personal credibility. I was sending it to potential business angels so I selected people from the school database who were interested in angel investing, which I also added to the subject line.

In the body of the email I explain that I'm from the same school as them, that I've already invested in this company, and I give plenty of information about the business idea – what stage it's at, the industry area, etc. At the end I ask if I can send more information to them.

Below is another example of a great introductory email. This time I was on the receiving end.

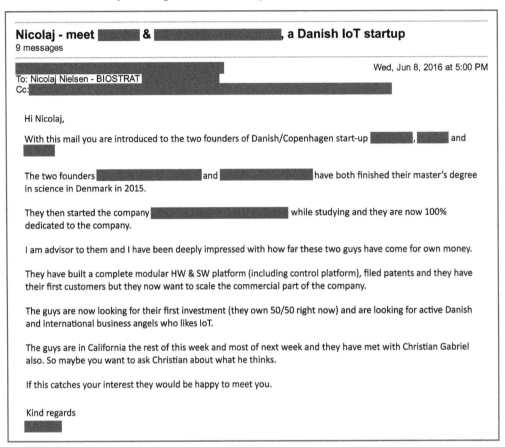

.This is a great example for many reasons:

1. The sender was a trusted contact of mine, and not just a random person. Søren is a former VC who I know well so this generates trust. This is supported by the fact Søren explains he is also acting as an advisor for the startup.

2. Søren then explains about the startup/founders to make me more interested: they are in Denmark (great – close by), they are full-time (great – committed!), and their startup is relevant to me (Internet of Tings) looking for business angel financing).

3. Finally, he mentions that we have a mutual contact (Christian) who also knows the founders, making it easy for me to research who they are.

This opening email simply asks if I'm interested and is a classic example of an email sent to potential business investors.

If they say yes, now you need to provide a little more information – your executive summary.

 © 2017 Nicolaj Højer Nielsen

Key note: Don't ask the investor to sign an NDA on the first date!

One of the classic mistakes made by startups when contacting investors is to ask them to sign a non-disclosure agreement (NDA) at first contact. The entrepreneurs are concerned the investor will steal their fantastic idea, but the problem is that 99 per cent of professional investors won't sign an NDA that early in the investment process! Investors get hundreds of proposals per year, and many of them contain similar business ideas. If you end up in detailed discussions and due diligence with a specific investor, they might be willing to sign a NDA once you are sharing sensitive data about your business. But they won't sign on the first date!

Start by making them interested in your project by spending the first meeting on presenting non-confidential data to them, and spare the remaining one per cent of information that's really sensitive until later in the process. And remember – all professional investors are in the trust business. If it is known in the startup community that they share confidential data, they will lose their reputation straight away!

Step 2 – The executive summary

By now you hopefully have the attention of a potential investor. They have received the basic information in your first email via a trusted contact. Now what kind of material should you send?

I suggest you send a very brief document in the form of an executive summary. This should be a one-pager describing your company and the opportunity it presents for the investor. Remember, you're not trying to get an investment, you just want to get them interested so you can proceed to the next step. The goal with the executive summary is to get a meeting, in person or by conference call.

The summary can either be sent as an attachment to the introductory email (coming from you or the mutual contact) to the investor, or alternatively in the next step after the investor has responded and indicated initial interest.

Again, don't send a 50-page business plan. It's information overload and the potential investor will never read it. You might need to send them something more elaborate later, but at this stage send them something brief they will actually read. The second reason is that a one-page executive summary makes you focus; you must be very precise in what you communicate.

Below is an example of an executive summary from a company I co-founded.

CODESEALER
Protecting online banking

Reducing online bank fraud without irritating the end-users

Industry: IT-security software

Key IP: Three patents concerning novel obfuscation technologies and validation of web pages using JavaScripts

Product: The world's first invisible Web Session Firewall that does not require any end-user action or client installation

Customers and business model: Financial institutions, recurring software licensing fees

Status: Product launched in Dec 2011. Three banks signed as pilot-customers (total of 20 million users)

Company: Located in Copenhagen, Denmark. 12 FTEs.

Current investors: SEED Capital (DK), business angels and founders ($2.5 million in total)

Investment opportunity: $5 million in Q4 2012 to accelerate sales and marketing

Key Team Members:

▮▮▮▮▮▮▮▮CEO
Serial entrepreneur,10 years' experience in commercialization of technology products

▮▮▮▮▮▮▮▮CTO
15 years' experience within cryptography and IT-security consultant to several banks

▮▮▮▮▮VP Sales
Highly experienced in sales of IT-security products to EU banks

Forecast: Cash-flow positive by Q2 2013. By 2015 the company will protect 175 million users, have yearly revenue of $90 million and EBITDA margins of +60%.

The pain. Half of the world's computers are infected with viruses that cyber criminals use to commit online bank fraud. The direct losses are $3-4 billion per year and growing with +20 % p.a. Banks have no effective measures against the attacks. The current solutions demand the active involvement of the end-users leading to very high implementation and maintenance costs, inconvenience for the end-users and lack of compliance.

CodeSealer's solution. The world's first <u>invisible</u> software based Web Session Firewall that does not require any end-user action or client installation. It enables financial institutions to reduce direct and indirect costs of malware-based mobile- and online bank fraud.

The product is installed on the bank's servers and works by establishing a secure session between the user's browser and the Web Session Firewall. The product continuously monitors the web pages displayed to the end-user to detect unauthorized changes. All communication with the user's browser is encrypted and authenticated using session-specific cryptographic keys. The unique obfuscation and verification technologies are protected by three patents.

CodeSealer's approach is unique. A) We are protecting the bank's entire online bank user-base without annoying them! B) We are <u>not</u> trying to remove the malware, but instead detecting whenever it tries to break into the online bank and C) The solution is browser independent and works on both PCs, macs, tablets and smartphones.

The market. The addressable market is the approx. $3 billion banks are spending on two-factor authentication systems, to which CodeSealer's solution is a strong complement. The main geographical market has so far been EU, but the use of two-factor authentication is rapidly spreading to USA (driven by new regulation) and Asia (driven by rapid increase in online banking). The current global 1 billion online bank users will have increased to 2 billion users by 2015.

Traction. The first product has been released and has been launched in EU in November 2011. Three European banks with up to 20 million users have signed as pilot-customers with further ten banks in the pipeline (75 million users).

Partnership with IBM. CodeSealer has furthermore signed a non-exclusive partnership agreement with IBM, who has a very strong presence within the financial services sector. IBM will help market the product by testing the product and present the solution towards their clients.

More information. For additional information or to schedule a presentation detailing the opportunity please contact ▮▮▮▮▮▮▮ at ▮▮▮▮▮▮▮▮or ▮▮▮▮▮▮▮▮▮▮

This is a classic one-pager describing quite a nerdy company, CodeSealer, which makes very technical encryption software for banks. Immediately you can see how little focus there is on

 © 2017 Nicolaj Højer Nielsen

the technology. Let's look at the headline, which is the value proposition to banks: *Reducing online bank fraud without irritating the end users*. It's saying to banks, *decrease fraud and make your customers happy*. Then it talks about the customer problem: *there are a lot of cyber-attacks on banks*. The solution and what's unique: *doesn't require the end user to do anything*. The market: *big enough as banks are spending three billion dollars a year on similar technologies*. Then on to traction: *quite far, with partnerships*. On the left-hand side, the one-pager sums up key points; how far they have got, that they are a Danish company, how many people they have working for them, their investors and team members. A single page describes the company and gives answers to the questions investors typically pose before considering their next step.

Step 3 – The pitch deck

So you've been invited to the next step; either a physical meeting or conference call with the potential investor. Now you need the pitch deck – a set of 10 to 15 slides that explain your business in more detail. It's important to realise that the investor won't make a decision after that pitch; you won't get the money right away. You are just looking to take the process one step further.

 Key note: Get to the point – investors spend three minutes on your pitch deck!

One of the classic mistakes entrepreneurs make is to develop way-too-long pitch decks with up to 50 slides. This bores the audience when presenting the slides. But you often you need to send the slides. out beforehand (to get the potential investor interested in meeting you).

So how long does the average investor spend on reading the slide-deck you have spent days and days to develop? According to a study done by the company DocSend, three minutes and 44 seconds!

Conclusion: Get to the point – fast – in your pitch decks!

They will probably ask you to send the slides to them afterwards, and then they'll discuss your pitch internally and maybe send it to external parties for their opinion. That's why it's important that these slides (your pitch deck) are self-explanatory so they can be used by people who didn't attend the call or meeting. They have to be stand-alone because you might have a call with a junior at the company who needs to pass the slides and their opinion on to more senior members of the investment team.

What needs to be in the pitch deck?

If you talk with 10 different investors they will give you 10 different ways to organise their slides. It's very subjective, and to some it's almost a religion. What I propose here in terms of the 15 or so slides that any investor would like to see is quite mainstream. You can change the order around, but this is the basic content you need to have in your deck.

Please note that your pitch deck might be 15 slides but never 30 or 50 slides! You simply won't have the time to go through all the slides since on average you will be asked to present your company in approximately 15 to 20 minutes.

The typical content of a pitch deck

DocSend analysed the content of the pitch decks from 200 different startups. On average there were 19 slides with the content shown below:

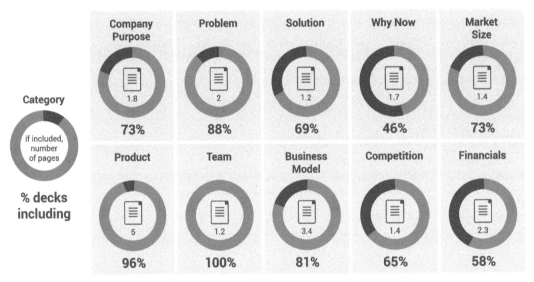

Source: DocSend

Real life examples of pitch decks that worked

The following examples use real-life pitch slides from companies I have been involved in. These slides have led to success in getting funding from business angels, public funds and venture capital funds. They are taken from four very different types of companies – one SaaS (Capdesk), one consumer electronics (Recon Instruments), one biotech company (Motility-Count), and one cyber-security company (Sepior). To put the slides into perspective you will find a brief introduction to the four companies below:

 © 2017 Nicolaj Højer Nielsen

Company name	Brief description
Capdesk	Capdesk is online software (SaaS) aimed at private companies and their investors. Capdesk is a shareholder management tool that makes it easier for companies to manage their investors, for investors to be updated on progress in the company, and for investors to trade these shares in unlisted companies. Capdesk was founded in 2015 and the pitch deck used here is from the business angel funding in 2015-2016.
Recon Instruments	Recon Instruments is a consumer electronics company. Their first product was ski goggles with a built-in head-up-display (computer screen) and later a sunglasses version. The company was founded in 2007 and sold to Intel in 2015. The pitch deck used here is from 2009 when the company was looking for business angel and/or venture capital funding.
MotilityCount	MotilityCount is a biotech company. Their first product was a male fertility test (sperm quality test) for home use. The company was founded in 2010, and the pitch deck used here is from the first investment round in 2011 where business angels and public funds invested in the company.
Sepior	Sepior is a cyber security company. Their first product is an encryption solution that protects cloud services (Dropbox, Gmail etc.) from being hacked. The pitch deck used here is from the seed/venture round in 2015 and 2016.

Slide 1 – Introduction

The first slide gives you the opportunity to explain what your business is all about in one sentence. Capdesk is 'a market for the world's unlisted shares', MotilityCount is 'a point-of-care male fertility checker' and Recon Instruments says 'we develop wearable near-to-eye display and content solutions for fast paced environments'.

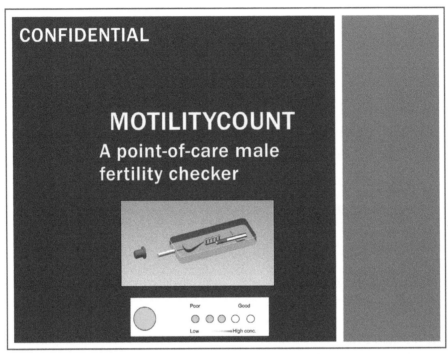

 © 2017 Nicolaj Højer Nielsen

All these companies would have benefitted from adding basic contact information at the bottom of the first slide: website address, email, name of contact person etc.

The biggest mistake in the introduction is not being clear and concise when it comes to telling the audience what you're doing. Or as Lars Andersen, General Partner at SEED Capital explains:

I have seen thousands of pitches, and the most common mistake startups make is that they forget to explain, short and sweet, what it is they do. Tell me in one or two sentences what you do and why. Lunar Way nailed it when they pitched for us. They said: 'Seventy-one per cent of millennials would rather go to the dentist than listen to their bank – we are mobile banking for millennials'. You want to leave the listener with a 'no brainer' reaction.

Slide 2 – The team

One of the most important parts of your slide-deck is information about your team. Remember, early-stage investing is about building trust; you need to build trust in your team and show you have the skills. Say who you are and what you've done in the past.

Jakob Ekkelund, former venture capitalist, says:

The team is everything. I (and all professional investors) would any day choose a killer team with a 'bad idea' compared to a so-so team with a fabulous idea. Many startups fail in making a credible story with regards to the team having the needed skills and experience to succeed with the specific startup, especially in regards to having the practical experience actually doing it. Hands-on experience eats academic degrees for breakfast! In other words, professional investors would rather invest in a person with a first degree and tons of hands-on marketing experience rather than someone with a PhD in marketing but no practical experience.

You need to demonstrate that you have at least two basic skill sets at your company; the makers and the sellers. If you're making a product, show who's going to make it. You also need someone who can sell, not just to customers, but someone who can build external relationships and partnerships. The third thing you preferably need to show (in both the makers and the sellers) is industry expertise. If you're solving a problem in a particular industry and you have no one on your team who has experience working in that industry, it's a hard sell to investors. Imagine you want to sell computer games and none of the developers, even though they're good programmers, nor you as the sales guy, have ever worked with computer games.

You don't need to demonstrate a team that is perfect for the long run because investors know that in five years your team will look different. They need to be convinced that you have the team in place that will deliver on the next milestone.

Some people prefer to have the slide about the team at the start of the pitch deck since the team's background will give credibility to the arguments made later in the slide-deck (I'm one of those people). Others prefer to have it at the end of the slide-deck to wrap up the presentation.

Below is an example of a team slide. You'll see that the company has four founders. Christian and Casper, who work in the specific crowd funding industry, demonstrate they have the commercial skills to understand this industry. There's also Mikkel and Martin, the technical guys on the team who have been working for 15 years developing software. Both have master's degrees and have worked in software development at one of Denmark's most well-respected

 © 2017 Nicolaj Højer Nielsen

companies. Finally, the slide includes information on the two first investors, Ivan and Nicolaj, to show they're experienced and give further credibility to the case.

Here's another example, this time from MotilityCount, the home-test device for male fertility (checking sperm quality). Since this is a project with a high degree of technical risk, it's important to give credibility to the technical team behind the invention (Steen and Jacob) on the team slide. But it's also essential to show that the startup has the needed competency to actually go out and commercialise the technology (Nicolaj).

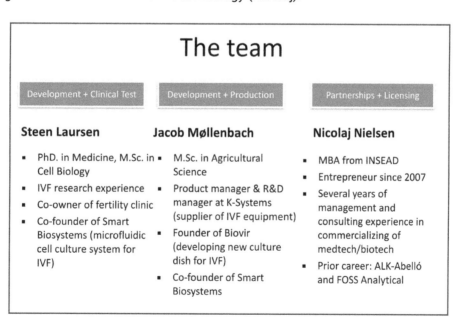

Christian Thaler-Wolski is a startup advisor who previously worked as a venture capitalist:

In SaaS, the team set-up at the very early-stage is pretty simple. In my view, you really only need two or three founders – one technologist and one product person. Maybe a business guy. Never a finance guy. One person should lead as CEO. Especially in Europe, I often see teams where 'everyone is equal'. Young first-time entrepreneurs, often of similar backgrounds, don't want to offend each other and want to share the burden of decision-making and eventual success which is fundamentally OK, but it doesn't really work. Typically, the guy who always talks to the investors ends up being the CEO. In a case where you have three or more founders, not everyone needs to be a managing director of the company; two are fine. In the UK and US in particular, investors like to talk to one person when they pick up the phone, not three. Which means the whole team doesn't need to take part in every investor call. It also shows me whether the rest of the team have confidence and trust in the CEO.

Slide 3 – The problem

Once you've presented your team, you need to explain the problem you're looking to solve in simple terms. Below you will see an example of a problem slide from MotilityCount. The storyline goes like this: *A lot of couples are having trouble getting pregnant, in many cases due to poor sperm quality. And if they want to get the male tested, they will have to visit a hospital which is inconvenient and embarrassing to do.* Note that the slide attempts to quantify the number of couples who have this problem in order to send a clear message to the investor – the problem is huge!

 © 2017 Nicolaj Højer Nielsen

Pain: Male infertility

Many couples are concerned about sperm quality

- 1/6 of all couples have to use In Vitro Fertilization to get pregnant
- Large part of infertility cases are linked to sperm quality
- USA: Population of 6-7 million women having problem getting pregnant*
- Denmark: 37.000 IVF treatments per year **
- Denmark: 8,5% of all babies are born with the help of IVF***

But need to visit specialty clinic or hospital to get answer

- No valid home-test on the market
- Couple will have to visit their doctor
- But doctor/GP can not test sperm quality, and will refer to IVF clinic/ hospital
- If not living close (less than 1 hour away) to hospital/clinic, sperm sample has to be produced at the site...

Very inconveniently, time consuming and embarrassing for men/ couples to know if he has poor sperm quality

* http://www.cdc.gov/reproductivehealth/infertility/#4
** http://www.sst.dk/Nyhedscenter/Nyheder/2012/Fertillitetsbehandlinger2010.aspx
*** http://fertilitetsselskab.dk/images/2013_dok/aarsmoedefiler2013/dfs2012.pdf

Another example of a problem slide is shown below, this time from Recon Instruments. Here the problem is explained using the lack of navigation, performance measurement and communication with friends when hitting the slopes. Please note that this slide is from 2009, before everyone had smartphones with unlimited data packages!

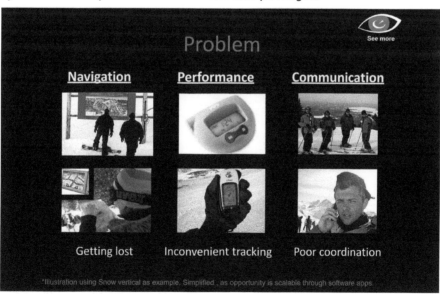

The final example is from Capdesk, explaining the problem that shareholders in private companies have a hard time getting liquidity due to relatively few IPOs, and it takes many years for

a startup to reach that point.

Problem

Slow IPO market and few private liquidity events

	1996	2015
IPO's	846	169
Average Age	4	8

🔒 Shareholders are locked to private companies

Slide 4 – Your solution

You've shown there's a problem, so what's your solution? A common mistake with the solution slide (especially among technical founders) is to provide too many technical details. It is all features, features, features: our device is 3.6% faster and 18% smaller than existing ones. Do customers care? The focus needs to be on user value. What is the value to them of using your product compared to that of existing products?

Below is Recon Instruments' solution-slide.

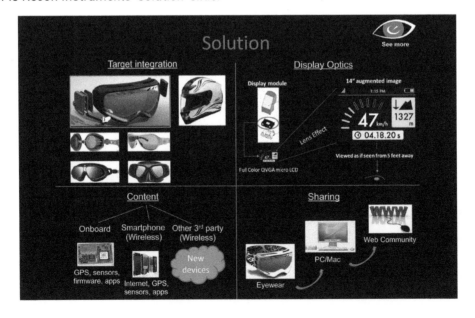

 © 2017 Nicolaj Højer Nielsen

This slide highlights what Recon Instruments believe is the best solution to the problem: ski goggles with a built-in computer screen that shows the skier the important data directly on the inside of the goggles.

Below is another example from MotilityCount, which shows the intended solution to the problem of lack of male fertility tests: a home test that gives an answer about sperm quality within an hour.

Solution and value proposition

An easy-to-use test-kit, which gives a fast and reliable answer on male fertility

- **Results:** Colour reaction (poor vs. normal sperm quality)
- **Privacy:** Eliminates the need to visit IVF specialist/hospital for (initial) testing
- **Convenience :** Can be bought at pharmacies, drugstores and online
- **Reliable:** Test results correlate strongly with golden standard (microscopy)
- **Fast:** Gives answer within 30-60 minutes
- **Easy to use:** No liquids to handle

Finally, Capdesk's solution slide:

Solution

Empower companies to facilitate **liquidity events**, while staying private

Note the lack of technical details in all the examples! This slide should be about the unique solution and the value to your customers, not the technical details behind it!

Slide 5 – Your unfair advantage

You've shown that you have a solution to a problem and the team to make that solution real and successful. Now you need to show your special skills – how you can solve this problem better than anyone else. This is your unfair advantage. What makes you special? Do you know something others don't? Do you have some intellectual property? Have you seen what others haven't and does that give you first-mover advantage? What is it? You need to tell.

Ekkelund explains what VCs are searching for:

All VCs are looking for cases who are building something that's hard for future competitors to copy. Many startups fail to communicate how they are planning to build such defensibility. Such defence can come in many forms, and first-time entrepreneurs especially often think 'patents/trademarks' where this is seldom the key perceived defence mechanism, especially within IT. What really turns on VCs are network effects – where the value of your product/service becomes higher and higher for the customers as more and more are using it (think companies like LinkedIn, Facebook etc.) If your startup can generate such network effects, will it be really hard for any competitor to enter the market? This makes VCs really interested!

The big mistake I see is relying too much on patents. Technical founders in particular believe this is the only way to protect the market, but many experienced investors are cynical about the value of patents as many can be bypassed. Make sure you do not rely only on your patents when you describe your unfair advantage!

The example below is from Sepior, a cyber security company, and includes the intellectual property (patent strategy). Please note patents only play a minor role in this slide and the focus is more on the hard-to-replicate know-how Sepior has within this specific technology.

 © 2017 Nicolaj Højer Nielsen

Our secret source

Know how

- Leaders within Secure Multiparty Computation (SMC)
- The first in the world to have commercialized SMC
- Commercial SMC applications dependent on *both* speed of algorithms & knowledge of practical use
  - Our general-purpose algorithms are the worlds fastest
  - Special-purpose algorithms tailored to key management (otherwise SMC not feasible!)

IP strategy

- Patenting specific parts of the KMaaS solution, making it even harder to enter for potential future competitors

Unique and hard to replicate know how, built upon +20 years of university research

Slide 6 – The competitive landscape

A big mistake amongst founders is to believe they have no competitors, when it is most likely they have indirect competitors solving the same problem in a different way. If you take MotilityCount, there's no-one out there with the exact same technology because it's patented, but there will be others who've tried to solve the same problem using different technologies. If you can't find anyone who's solved the same problem, maybe you should ask if there's really a problem to be solved.

Let's take a look at Recon Instruments.

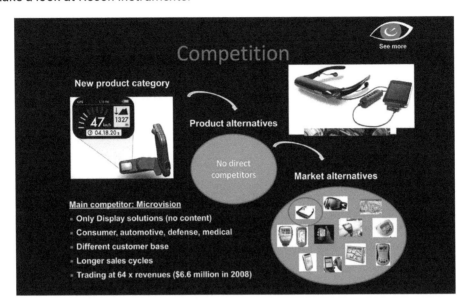

From this slide you can see that this is a new product category. At the time, no-one else had made a head-up display like this and there was no direct competition. But of course there were market alternatives and these are shown in the slide. The slide also lists the main competitors. Recon Instruments show their market knowledge, acknowledge that there are alternatives, and demonstrate how they are different.

Another example is the slide from Sepior, which shows the trade-off with existing solutions, and thereby the benefit of Sepior.

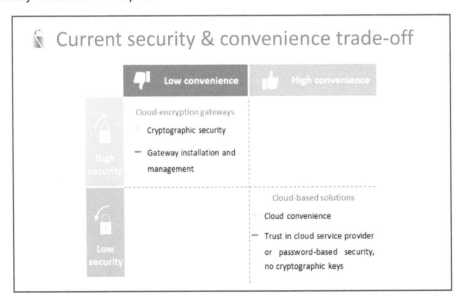

 © 2017 Nicolaj Højer Nielsen

If you are in a market which is more developed and has more competitors, it might make sense to be more specific regarding how you are different from your competitors. This can be done as a matrix like the slide below from Capdesk.

Slide 7 – Business model

It's important to realise that for the specific problem you are solving with your product, there can be multiple business models. Therefore you need to provide the potential investor with an overview about how you intend to make money with your product.

Recon Instruments had invented a technology that enabled them to build computer screens and network connection into goggles. Whether they should sell it directly to consumers or partner up with existing players are just two important questions to consider in their business model. In the end, Recon decided to team up with existing sport equipment players.

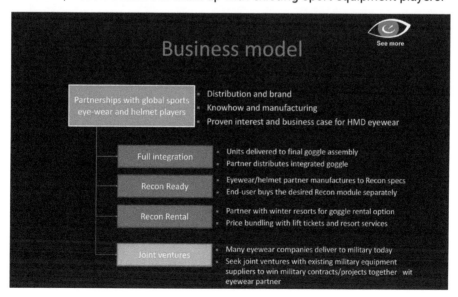

Capdesk were in the same situation: in building software connecting investors and companies, how should that product be monetised? Who should pay for what? Capdesk decided that the basic use of the software should be free for both investors and companies and they would only charge money when shares switched hands.

Business Model

Price per transaction:

Minimum $100   Maximum 0,5%

Slide 8 – Traction

You've convinced the investor that there's a major problem and you can solve it, you have the right team and the best business model. It's now time to show how much you have accomplished. You've already learnt in this book that no-one invests in an idea, so it's important for you to show how much you have already accomplished.

The slide below from Capdesk was used in early June 2016 to showcase what they had done in less than a year with limited funding. They built the product, launched it, got a lot of users, and got acquisition offers.

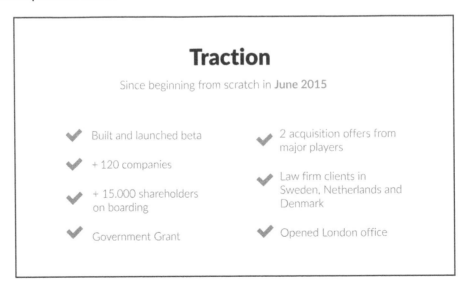

 © 2017 Nicolaj Højer Nielsen

Another example below is from Recon Instruments (2009) in which they have highlighted what they achieved on both the R&D and market sides.

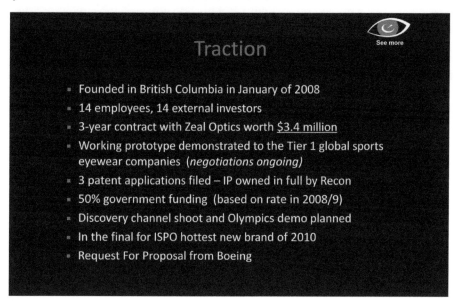

Slide 9 – The market

Let's assume you can solve a major problem and customers like your product, but it turns out there are only a hundred customers in the world. One of the biggest fears many investors have is of ending up in too small a market. That's why you need to demonstrate that the market is big enough for a profitable company based on a reasonable share of that market.

Or as Jakob Ekkelund explains:

It's essential that the person at the receiving end of the pitch gets the feeling that the start-up is entering a really big market. At a minimum, you need to communicate that the market might be small now but it has the potential to become really large. No one wants to invest in a small and/or heavily declining market, because the investor knows that before your startup becomes successful – and later ready to exit – the market will be so small that the company will be worthless.

There are two different markets:

1. Your customers are already spending a lot of money on a similar product, it's easy to find a marketplace, and you can explain why you're able to take customers away from current vendors.

2. The market is new. Potential customers are not spending money on something that is solving the exact same problem, so it's hard to guess how big the market will be.

The first type of market is relatively simple to estimate; because there's an existing market it's relatively easy to quantify the total size. But many startups, especially innovative ones, fall into the second category. Customers aren't spending money on similar products which is why you believe there's a market opportunity. But how do you convince investors that there *is* a huge market opportunity when there's no market today?

MotilityCount is a good example of this. This is how the company presented the market potential for their product on sperm testing:

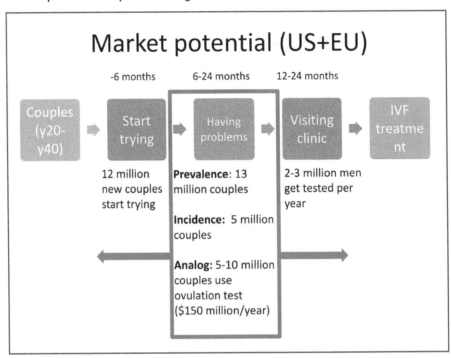

The problem is that over the past 20 years many companies have tried to launch sperm quality tests but none have been successful. The reasons are multiple and include the product not working and being difficult to use. In such cases, it's difficult to argue for a large market, so how do you do it? How can you explain that you still have a big enough potential market?

This slide explains how many potential customers there are in the EU and US, the target geographical market. *Every year 12 million new couples try to fall pregnant. Approximately five million of these experience problems. Many of them use an ovulation kit or have so much trouble that they get tested at a fertility clinic.* These numbers show there is a market with five million potential new customers a year who are willing to spend money on solving this problem. In other words, instead of saying directly that the market for sperm quality tests today is large (which it's not), we say it will become large since the number of people who have the problem is high and they have already proved they are willing to spend money on solving the problem, albeit with products from a different product category (ovulation tests).

 © 2017 Nicolaj Højer Nielsen

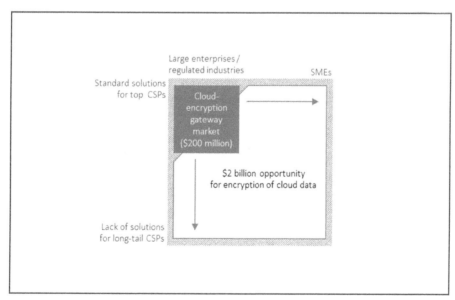

Market Size

$250B

*excluding Natural Resources, Real Estate, Infrastructure

Private Equity Capital Raised in 2015
(Bain & Company 2016)

Another example is from Capdesk, who use the private equity market as a benchmark, and thereby imply how much potential there is in the future for transfers of unlisted shares.Finally, Sepior uses a mixture of strategies. First they state the existing market trying to fix the same problem is $200 million per year, but that Sepior can make this market grow 10-fold by having many more types of content providers and enterprises using it compared to the existing solutions.

Large enterprises /
regulated industries   SMEs

Standard solutions
for top CSPs

Cloud-
encryption
gateway
market
($200 million)

$2 billion opportunity
for encryption of cloud data

Lack of solutions
for long-tail CSPs

Slide 10 – Go to market

Now you need a slide explaining how you're going to enter the market with your product. What's your marketing/distribution channel or strategy? What investors are you looking for? How can you best go to market in a timely and cost-effective way?

Because you're a small startup with limited resources, you can't do it like IBM or Google would. So what's your plan for tapping into what you believe is a big market for your great product? Will you target customers directly or via partners? Offline or online? What kind of product will they buy if your product is only part of the value proposition?

A common mistake for B2C startups is assuming your customers will start coming almost by themselves – on an almost non-existing marketing budget. In 99 per cent of cases this doesn't happen. For each Angry Birds, there are a hundred thousand other game developers who have tried and failed. How are you going to get all these users on board on a limited budget? What's your marketing strategy? Are there any analogies you can use to show companies who have done it in a similar way? Do you have the skills to do it?

Another common mistake is assuming that after you sign up partners they'll do the selling for you. This is often the case in software for enterprise companies who find partners in each country and assume they will do the selling so there won't be any marketing costs. But partners are notoriously bad at launching new products. They're good at taking an existing success and scaling it – but don't rely on them for launching.

One example of such a slide is below from MotilityCount, explaining the two potential go-to-market strategies for their product (and that one of them would require further capital):

GO-TO-MARKET STRATEGIES

PLAN A
- Licensing agreement with major OTC player in 2012
- Sales and marketing to be done by partner
- No further capital will be needed

PLAN B
- Bring the product to the market
- In collaboration with independent distributors
- More capital will be needed in 2013
- Long term strategy will remain the same (Plan A)

An alternative is the way Sepior did it, explaining in detail (with financials) the two different

 © 2017 Nicolaj Højer Nielsen

routes to the market for their product – direct and via partners – for the two different customer segments:

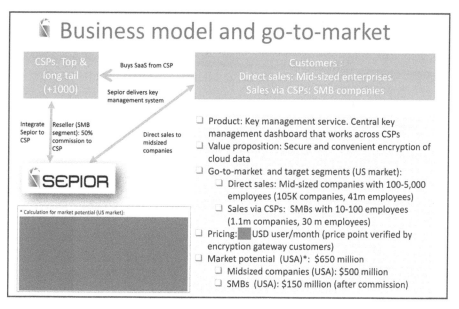

Slide 11 – Financials

How much money are we all going to make? Now the time has come for the slide about your future projections. The common approach is the classic hockey stick to financial forecasting: 'We're not making money now but in five years' time we'll be filthy rich.' Be realistic. Optimism is great, but you need to be able to defend your figures. If you're saying you'll make 20 million in five years, you'll need to show how that fits your 'go-to market' strategy and the money you're asking for from investors. And all this needs to be based on your budget.

Or as Søren Jessen Nielsen, former partner at two VC funds, says:

You should avoid presenting long-term financial forecasts that are very precise down to several digits: 'In 2018 our revenue will be €4,213,452 with a profit of €256,714.' No-one will take such calculations seriously, and it shows a lack of understanding of financial forecasts in a startup with an extreme degree of uncertainty. Focus instead on the overall business model with a few different scenarios on how different degrees of success/growth will impact the future financial. Be honest but bold in your expectations, and also remember to discuss the potential issues the case has from a financial point of view. Remember, a VC partner develops a very sophisticated BS filter after having heard thousands of pitches from startups, and the ability to communicate both the positive and the potential challenges will give you a lot of credibility compared to companies that offer slides filled with BS and buzzwords.

The biggest mistake here is not stating your assumptions. You come up with a pretty hockey stick, but you don't include the number of customers it's based on, how much money they pay, and how you get those customers. The numbers will be meaningless. The investor can't really judge whether they're valid or not.

Below is an example from MotilityCount, stating both the expected outcome in terms of revenue and profit and the key drivers and assumptions.

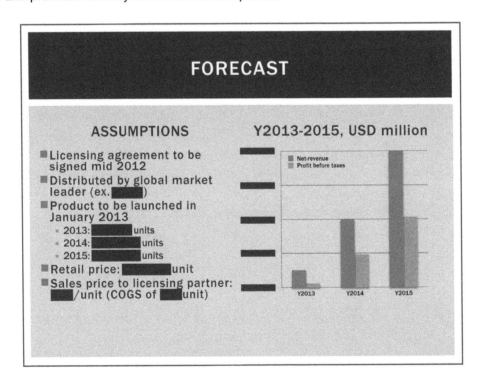

 © 2017 Nicolaj Højer Nielsen

An alternative version is the one below from Recon Instruments:

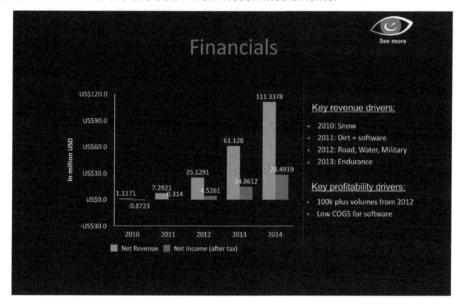

The biggest mistake when startups pitch: missing numbers

Niels Henrik Rasmussen, serial entrepreneur and business angel says:

It's fair that you're driven by your vision and overall hypothesis on the market, and demand for your product, but you must include figures in the pitch! Explain your reasoning and underlying assumptions about how you will develop your business and the impact on your financials. I fully understand the uncertainties involved in such forecasting and know the estimated figures are likely to change, but you need to do your best. How can I evaluate if the business is viable or not if you aren't trying to put figures on it?

Slide 12 – Milestones

You've presented the long-term vision and now you have to talk short-term milestones; the next-step plan for the near future. One mistake startups make is not having a detailed plan for the next steps. It makes investors nervous when they can't see the internal milestones. In

90 per cent of cases you won't get the money for the next three years all up front, you'll get it in tranches (phased funding). And investors need to see how you plan to spend that money.

Let's continue with an example from MotilityCount, with their milestones (and spending) for the upcoming phases.

DEVELOPMENT ROADMAP

	FINAL PROTOTYPE:	PRESALES MODEL:	SALES MODEL:
Product development	-Device and size optimized to reduce test time -Cells stained at inlet	-Finalize design and functionality -Test of device outside project group (IVF clinics and sperm-banks)	-Optimize design based upon feedback from external tests -International tests (IVF clinics and sperm-banks)
Milestones	-Test time <1 hour - Test results comparable to CASA studies (Computer Assisted Sperm Analysis)	-Test time <30 minutes -Closed system with semi-automatic loading of fluids and cells -Positive clinical tests	-Production cost less than $10/unit -Roadmap to reduce costs to $4/unit -Positive clinical tests -Signing of licensing agreement
Timing	6 months	9 months	6 months
Costs	DKK 1.5 million	DKK 2.5 million	DKK 2 million

There are three phases going from where they are now to a prototype, from a prototype to a pre-sales model, and then to something that's tested and can be sold to customers. The company believes each phase will take six to nine months and have shown expected costs based on this belief. This is a good way to show investors that along with a long-term high-flying vision, you also have a detailed strategy for the following periods – because this is what they're going to fund.

If you have a more developed product already on the market, your development roadmap may show how you are going to go from five to 200 customers and from 200 to 2000 customers.

 © 2017 Nicolaj Højer Nielsen

Advice on communicating to VCs: Think both long and short term!

Dan Eisenhardt, co-founder of the Vancouver Founder Fund, says:

As an early-stage venture fund partner, the biggest mistake I see entrepreneurs make is that they either don't have a strong enough vision or they have too big a vision without enough specificity and focus. Both these mistakes are equally bad and will make us reject the offer to invest almost immediately.

Not having a big enough vision is a problem because it's not something we as a VC can teach or inject. It has to come from the founder. Thinking too big early on without enough focus shows the founder hasn't done their homework properly and doesn't know how to prioritise in order to get traction and differentiate from competitors.

The right approach is to be bold and visionary but have a very specific entry point to get maximum traction with core users before adding features or broadening the market. This shows the entrepreneur can think strategically and is realistic about what can be achieved. It will also greatly reduce the resource draw and time to market – both very important things for VCs when evaluating risk. But it's important the founder has a clear path to scaling up the business based on the market validation. That is sometimes difficult as it can seem overwhelming to plan several steps ahead when so many things need to get done just to deliver the minimum viable product to the early adopters.

Without this short and long term approach, the plan for the business won't be meaningful, and assessing the return and risk profile becomes problematic.

Slide 13 – The ask

The ask slide is all about how much money you are looking for and what you'll give in return. It's critical that you show how far the money you are asking for will take you. Will the financing take you all the way to a profitable company? How far will it take you? Many startups make the mistake of not including this information.

Below is an example from Recon Instruments who state how much funding the company have already secured in the past, how much the company is asking for now, and the main use of this money.

An alternative is the slide below from Sepior, stating the intended use of the proceeds, and the milestones it will enable the company to achieve:

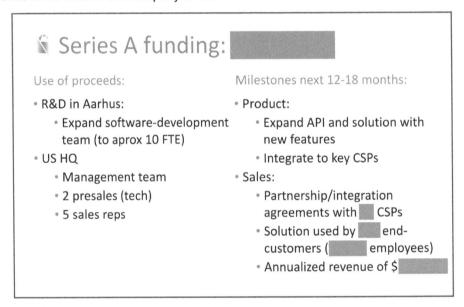

Slide 14 – Summary

Finally, summarise why the investor should invest.

The Capdesk slide below is a great example. This slide sums up that they believe they have a great team, they already have satisfied customers, they're growing really fast, there's a large market, and there is a clear exit opportunity because the first companies have already approached them.

Many s end their presentation to investors with a Q&A slide. Don't make that mistake. It's best

 © 2017 Nicolaj Højer Nielsen

to end on the summary slide and leave that slide up during the Q&A part of the meeting. This way every time they look up, they'll be reminded why they should invest.

Why Capdesk?

1. Ambition, team and technology to impact a $250B market

2. Scaleable
1 company = 200 shareholders
200 shareholders = 10 company invites

3. Born global
Users from all over the world

4. Exit Opportunities
Exchanges, Investment Banks, Transfer Agents, Investment Platforms, Payment providers etc.

Getting to the next step

The point of the first email, the executive summary, and the pitch deck is to ultimately get funding for your startup. Each step leads to the next. The purpose of the first contact email is to be invited to send the executive summary. The purpose of the executive summary is to get the investor to want to see the pitch deck. The pitch deck is to persuade them to fund your startup. If they say 'no' at any of these stages, what do you do then?

You ask for feedback. Perhaps the material is unclear. Perhaps you've selected the wrong investor and it's not their focus. If it's unclear, get feedback on what they don't understand. It could be a problem with your presentation skills or that the investors think you oversold the material. Many will say 'no' because they don't believe in your startup. As with any disruptive product, there will be a lot of people who don't agree with you. That is just how it is. People are different and see the world differently.

Take-away points

There are three types of basic materials needed to contact investors. The first is your initial contact material which you will likely send via email. It needs to summarise – very briefly – what your business idea is and why the investor should take the next step, i.e. what's in it for them. You then need an executive summary with enough details to get the investor hooked and interested in a meeting. This is sent after the investor has asked for it. You also need a more extensive presentation that can either be sent or presented in person.

Make it brief. Each type of material sent has one goal – getting to the next step with the investor. You don't close the deal on the first contact.

Wrap up – What next?

Whilst you can't fund an idea, ideas are of course what should drive you.

A great idea and ambition is not enough to get on in business. Investors know that, so don't waste your time and money trying to get an idea funded by external investors at the idea stage. Start by doing what all entrepreneurs have to do – put in the resources yourself, bootstrap and invest your own time and money, thereby proving you really want the startup to succeed.

You can't build a business on your own and your co-founders will not be just employees but the first investors in the company, since you most likely don't have the money to pay them a fair salary. They invest their time and get part of the upside in the form of equity. Then you and your co-founders will go out, verify the potential, and start building the business.

You and your team might run out of money before you make enough progress to attract professional investors. The solution for most startups? Ask friends and family members to invest in your startup, but beware of the risk of ruining friendships by doing so. And don't accept money from friends or family members who don't understand the huge risk they are taking!

At this point you may have reached a time where it makes sense to contact professional investors. Do your research and contact relevant investors; those who are interested in your type of business and who invest in the stage your company is at now. If you don't you will spend too much time talking to irrelevant investors!

If you're lucky, or smart, you won't need investors. If you and your team have gathered so much momentum in the market, you can live from the revenue you get from your customers instead of looking for external investors.

But even if you come to a point where your company is fundable, you should think twice before taking investors into the company. You should ask yourself: *Do we really need the money? Will the money make a tremendous difference to our company? Could the company live without it? Do we really need the money now, or could it wait until later?*

It's really hard to find entrepreneurs who regret they didn't take in external investors earlier in the journey, but it's easy to find entrepreneurs who regret taking in investors too early, when in hindsight they realise they could have bootstrapped longer.

Why do they regret it? In many cases because they now know the huge value jumps a startup takes when reaching new milestones. Where the value of an 'idea' is close to zero, the value skyrockets as the startup builds a team and prototype, launches a product, gets revenue, and starts to grow rapidly.

The first money you take in is very expensive since the value of your company is very low. If you end up taking too much money too early, you might end up owning only a small fraction of your company at exit. And this not only impacts your financial upside, but also your ability to be in control of your company.

 © 2017 Nicolaj Højer Nielsen

Select Bibliography

Steve Blank and Bob Dorf, *The Startup Owner's Manual: The Step-By-Step Guide for Building a Great Company,* K & S Ranch, 2012.

Rob Fitzpatrick, *The Mom Test: How to talk to customers and learn if your business is a good idea when everyone is lying to you,* Create Space, 2013.

Ash Maurya, *Running Lean: Iterate from Plan A to a Plan That Works,* O'Reilly Media, 2012.

John Mullins and Randy Komisar, *Getting to Plan B: Breaking Through to a Better Business Model,* Harvard Business School Press, 2009.

Eric Ries, *The Lean Startup: How Constant Innovation Creates Radically Successful Businesses,* Crown Business, 2011.

Noam Wasserman, *The Founder's Dilemmas: Anticipating and Avoiding the Pitfalls That Can Sink a Startup*, Princeton University Press, 2012.

Testimonials

Getting a startup actually started, funded, and then operational is not for the faint of heart. It's a complex and generally daunting process. Nicolaj's "The Startup Funding Book" is your go-to and how-to manual for navigating your path in building a startup you can be proud of. As an entrepreneur myself, I can say the book needs to be on your list of required reading!

- Shomit Ghose, Managing Director & Partner at Onset Ventures

"Nicolaj was instrumental in getting Recon Instruments off the ground. As one of its first shareholders, he led the first angel round and subsequently helped raise millions of dollars from angel investors around the world, using his network and expertise to identify people that would invest in what seemed to be a crazy idea at the time. His personal drive and ability to simplify and drive clarity was hugely beneficial in navigating the sometimes complex process of early-stage fundraising. I strongly urge entrepreneurs to follow his pragmatic advice in this book. It will get you results."

- Dan Eisenhardt, co-founder of Recon Instruments

 © 2017 Nicolaj Højer Nielsen

"When I read business books, I normally set out to highlight everything I find important in it with a yellow marker. I drop some books half way because I have marked almost nothing. I read others to the end because I frequently find important passages to mark up. And then occasionally I read books where I have to stop using the marker, since I would otherwise need to paint most of the book yellow. Nicolaj's book falls in this third category. It is extremely concise and practical, and I would highly recommend it to anyone looking to raise capital for a startup company."

- Lars Tvede, investor, author and serial entrepreneur.

"Nicolaj Nielsen shows you how to analyse what funding your venture needs and assesses the pros and cons of every major source. He then helps you reverse-engineer the way investors will think about financing your business and teaches you how to align your pitch with their mindsets. The section on how to find and work with a co-founder is worth the price of the book alone. Read this book before you start your business — its practical, intelligent advice could save you many months and missteps."

- Philip Anderson, INSEAD Alumni Fund Chaired Professor of Entrepreneurship

"My team and I have spent the last year developing our web and app platform and plan to grow the business through acquiring funding. Despite spending hours searching, I simply couldn't find a decent book on the different types of venture investment methods, let alone one aimed at an audience outside the US market. Fortunately, I stumbled on Nicolaj's website and signed up for the beta program to read his *Startup Funding* book. The depth and quality of information in the book has been extremely helpful in allowing us to better understand the various investment channels, as well as in clarifying our thoughts on which may be right for us and when. I would highly recommend this book to anyone with even a hint of entrepreneurial values in them."

- Andrew Ward, CTO of MODL App, CEO of Scorchsoft

 © 2017 Nicolaj Højer Nielsen

Lightning Source UK Ltd.
Milton Keynes UK
UKHW021002221020
371850UK00002B/127

9 788799 990207